Past imperfect

EDITORIAL

47(01): 1/3 | DOI: 10.1177/0306422018769574

by **Rachael Jolley**

Access to knowledge about history is being manipulated around the world to build political support, says **Rachael Jolley**

AUTHORITARIAN LEADERS KNOW their history. They also know the history they would like you to know. They are aware, perhaps more than anyone else, that choosing images and stories from the past to align and amplify the ways a country is run can be a terribly powerful tool.

As Canadian historian Margaret MacMillan discussed with Index for this issue, dictators have been aware of the power of history to make their arguments for centuries. From the first Chinese emperors to today's leaders – China's Xi Jinping and Turkey's Recep Tayyip Erdogan, among others – the selection of historical stories which reflect their view of the world is revealing.

"The thing about history is if people know only one version then it seems to validate the people in power," said MacMillan.

But if you know more, you can use that information to make informed decisions about what worked in the past – and what didn't – allowing people to learn and move on.

And right now, historical validation is an active part of the political playbook. In Russia, Vladimir Putin is a big fan of the tale of the great and powerful Russia. And what he doesn't like are people who don't sign up to his version of history.

Even asking questions about the past can provoke anger at the top. It interferes with the control, you see.

In 2014, Dozhd TV had an audience poll about whether Leningrad should have surrendered to the Nazis during World War II. Immediately there were complaints, as Index reported at the time. The station changed the wording of the question almost immediately, but within months various cable and satellite companies had dropped Dozhd from their schedules. Question and you shall be pushed out into the cold.

From the start, this magazine has covered how different countries have attempted to control the historical knowledge their citizens receive by limiting the pipeline (rewriting textbooks or taking history off the syllabus completely, for instance); using social pressure to make certain views taboo; and, in extreme cases, locking up historians or making them too afraid to teach the facts.

In our Winter 2015 issue, we covered the story of a Palestinian teacher who took his students to visit Nazi concentration camps in Poland because he felt they should know about the Holocaust. But not everyone agreed. While he was on the trip, there were demonstrations against him, his office was stormed and his car was torched. Later there were threats against his family. To escape the danger, he and his family had to move abroad. The teacher, Mohammed Dajani Daoudi, who wrote about his experiences for the magazine, said: "My duty as a teacher is to teach – to open new horizons for my students, to guide them out of the cave of misconceptions and see the facts, to break walls of silence, to demolish fences of taboos."

→

→ What an incredibly brave vision for a teacher to have in the face of a mob of people who would seek to damage his life, and that of his family, to show how much they disapproved of what he was trying to do.

Dajani Daoudi is not alone in fighting against the odds to bring research, open thinking and a wide base of knowledge to students. But, as our Spring 2018 issue shows, the odds are starting to stack up against people like him in an increasing number of places.

In 2010, Maureen Freely wrote a piece called Secret Histories for this magazine, about Turkish laws that had kept most of its citizens in the dark about the killings of a million Armenians in the last years of the Ottoman empire, and how those laws were enforced by making certain things – including criticising

The thing about history is if people know only one version, then it seems to validate the people in power

the legacy of modern Turkey's founding father, Mustafa Kemal Atatürk – illegal.

Turkey's government today has just passed a law making mention of the word "genocide" an offence in parliament, as our Turkish correspondent, Kaya Genç, reports on page 22.

But censoring history is not the only way to go about establishing inaccuracies and ill-informed attitudes about the past. Another option is to spin it.

Resisting Ill Democracies in Europe, the excellent report from the Human Rights House Network, acknowledges that a common thread in countries where democracy is weakening is the "reshaping of the historical narrative taught in schools". In Poland, the introduction of a Holocaust law means possible imprisonment for anyone who suggests Polish involvement in the Holocaust or

that the concentration camps were Polish. In Hungary, the rhetoric of the ruling party is to water down involvement of its citizens in the Holocaust and to rehabilitate the reputation of former head of state Miklós Horthy.

At the same time as undermining public trust in the media, governments in this spin cycle seek to stigmatise academics, as well as close down places where open or vigorous debate might take place. The result is often the creation of a "them and us" mentality, where belief in the avowed historical take is a choice of being patriotic or not.

As the HRHN report suggests, "space for critical thinking, independent research and reporting and access to objective and accurate information are pre-requisites for informed participation in pluralistic and diverse societies" and to "debunk myths".

However, if your objective is not having your myths debunked then closing down discussions and discrediting opposition voices is the ideal way to make sure the maximum number of people believe the stories you are telling.

That's why historians, like journalists, are often on the sharp end of a populist leader's attack. Creating a nostalgia for a time where supposedly the garden was rosy and citizens were happy beyond belief often forms another part of the political playbook, alongside creating a false history.

Another tactic is to foster a sense that the present is difficult and dangerous because of change and because of threats to "traditional" values; and a sense that history shows a country as greater than it is today. The next step is to find a handy enemy (migrants and LGBT people are often targets) to blame for that change and to stoke up anger.

Access to the past matters. Knowledge of what happened, the ability to question the version you are receiving, and probing and prodding at the whys and wherefores are essentials in keeping society and the powerful on their toes.

In this issue, we carry a special report

about how history is being abused. It includes interviews with some of the world's leading historians – Lucy Worsley, Margaret MacMillan, Charles van Onselen, Neil Oliver and Ed Keazor (p31).

We look at how history is being reintroduced into schools in Colombia (p60) and how efforts continue to recognise the victims of General Franco's dictatorship in Spain (p72). We also ask Hannah Leung and Matthew Hernon to talk to young people in China and Japan to discover what they learned at school about the contentious Nanjing massacre. Find out what happened on page 38.

Omar Mohammed, aka Mosul Eye, writes on page 47 about his mission to retain information about Iraq's history, despite risk to his life, while Isis set out to destroy historical icons.

And coming up… Don't miss our Index on Censorship podcast, with special guests, on Soundcloud @indexmagazine. ⊗

Rachael Jolley is editor of Index on Censorship. She tweets @londoninsider

ABOVE: A World War II veteran watches a guard marching at a memorial for victims of the war in Divnogorsk, Russia, 2015

CONTENTS

INDEX ON CENSORSHIP
VOLUME 47 NUMBER 01 – SPRING 2018

THE ABUSE OF HISTORY

THE POWERS BEING USED TO MANIPULATE THE PAST

CREDIT: Ben Jennings

IN FOCUS

CULTURE

BRITISH SOCIETY OF MAGAZINE EDITORS AWARDS 2016 WINNER

EDITOR
Rachael Jolley

DEPUTY EDITORS
Jemimah Steinfeld

SUB EDITORS
Jan Fox, Tracey Bagshaw, Sally Gimson, Adam Aiken

CONTRIBUTING EDITORS:
Irene Caselli, Jan Fox (USA), Kaya Genç (Turkey), Laura Silvia Battaglia

EDITORIAL ASSISTANT
Danyaal Yasin

ART DIRECTOR
Matthew Hasteley

COVER
Ben Jennings

THANKS TO:
Jodie Ginsberg, Sean Gallagher, Ryan McChrystal, Tracey Bagshaw, Georgia Hussey

Magazine printed by Page Bros., Norwich, UK

Index on Censorship | +44 (0) 20 7963 7262
292 Vauxhall Bridge Road, London SW1V 1AE, United Kingdom

Supported by
ARTS COUNCIL ENGLAND

SPECIAL REPORT

THE ABUSE OF HISTORY: THE POWERS BEING USED TO MANIPULATE THE PAST

MAIN: Russian servicemen take part in a military parade in Moscow's Red Square November, 2011, to mark the 70th anniversary of Soviet soldiers marching through the square towards the front lines during World War II

CREDIT: Jacques Langevin/Sygma/Getty

A date (not) to forget

47(01): 8/10 I DOI: 10.1177/0306422018770092

China has passed a law to make telling the wrong sort of history punishable. **Louisa Lim**, author of a book on the Tiananmen Square massacre, says she wouldn't be able to research her book today

TO WRITE THE People's Republic of Amnesia: Tiananmen Revisited, I spent a lot of time in fast-food restaurants. Not because I like burgers, but because dissidents often favour the crush of diners and the buzz of conversation, believing it complicates surveillance. As I sat in McDonald's with Bao Tong – who spent seven years in jail as the highest government official to be sentenced post-Tiananmen – he could point out which plainclothes policemen were shadowing him.

When I visited Zhang Xianling – who co-founded The Tiananmen Mothers, a group of relatives of those who died when the government troops crushed the democracy movement in Beijing on 4 June 1989 – her first words were: "They knew you were coming." The police had already phoned her to ask the purpose of my visit, knowledge presumably gleaned from tapping her, or my, phone. The surveillance was explicit by design: an act of intimidation aimed at multiple audiences.

My job, as a foreign correspondent for US radio station NPR, gave me reason to visit such interviewees, but even I became so paranoid that I kept my book a secret from my own children for months. I wrote, nervily, on a computer that had never been online, which I kept locked in a safe in my bedroom.

Today I would not be able to write the same book. Back in 2013 I did a crude survey on four Beijing university campuses, asking 100 students if they could identify the famous shot of Tank Man, the young white-shirted man facing down a column of tanks on the Avenue of Everlasting Peace. Of 100 students, only 15 knew where the photo had been taken. When a French camera crew repeated this exercise on a Beijing street a year later, it took only 10 minutes for the police to arrive. The journalists were interrogated for six hours. Nowadays it is hard to find anyone willing to speak to the foreign media on pretty much any topic, let alone one of the most politically sensitive episodes in China's recent history.

Under the leadership of President Xi Jinping – nicknamed the Chairman of Everything – even the past must be locked down. He spelled out why as he described the temporally all-encompassing nature of his key slogan, "The Chinese Dream is a dream about history, the present and the future." His dream of the "great rejuvenation of the Chinese nation" depends on the correct understanding of history, which is being imposed in an increasingly coercive fashion. To this end, new legislation passed last year introducing "historical nihilism" into the civil code ensures any independent questioning of official history bears increased risk, as well as potential financial costs. Nowadays, "encroaching upon the name, portrait, reputation and honour of heroes and martyrs" is a civil offence.

In their moves to suppress historical inquiry, China's 21st century rulers are following the path laid down by the country's first emperor, Qin Shihuang. In 213 BC he ordered all histories burned, except the official Qin records, in so thorough an act of intellectual destruction that even records of his own ancestry were destroyed. The aim, according to historian Sima Qian, writing more than 100 years later, was "to make the common people ignorant and to see to it that no one in the empire used the past to criticise the present". To underline that, in 210 BC the emperor is said to have buried a group of Confucian scholars alive for voicing criticism.

Today's equivalent of a live burial is a long prison sentence. Last year, activist Chen Yunfei was jailed for four years for "picking quarrels and stirring up trouble". His main offence? Visiting the grave of a Tiananmen victim. Four men who printed Tank Man labels for liquor bottles face long sentences for "inciting subversion of state power". Such sentences indicate that Tiananmen is becoming more – not less – sensitive over time.

In his 14th elegy to June Fourth, recently deceased Nobel laureate Liu Xiaobo wrote

Today's equivalent of a live burial is a long prison sentence

of "memory, severed by an eloquent depravity of speech":

For too long that secret
premeditated act has been repressed
locked within a magnificent lie.

Over the years, powerful figures like Alibaba's Jack Ma and Donald Trump, before he was US president, have voiced sympathy for China's brutal crackdown. Meanwhile, Beijing's success in amplifying its own version of history is writ large in absence: the fact that people died during the 1989 crackdown in Chengdu, the capital of Sichuan province, as well as in Beijing, was hardly written about until I uncovered details for my book (an arduous process, which involved relying on sources held outside China). As for those →

OPPOSITE: Beijing in the immediate aftermath of Tiananmen Square, June 1989. The numbers of dead are contested, but could have been as high as 10,000

ABOVE: People partake in a candlelit vigil in 2016 in Hong Kong on the Tiananmen anniversary

→ few Chinese accounts about the events in Beijing, they often contain verifiable falsehoods, even in university textbooks.

China's government archives are notoriously difficult to access, and getting more so. One picture posted recently by Harvard historian Michael Szonyi of the post-1949 Sichuan provincial archives summed it up: beside a sign reading "Open Catalogue" is a row of completely bare shelves. Nothing is open. Recent research by Hoover Institu-

Tiananmen matters, and to China's leaders it matters enough to mobilise the machinery of state

tion historian Glenn Tiffert indicates that Beijing is systematically censoring its electronic archive of Chinese academic journals to rectify sensitive periods of the past. This paucity of material – combined with fear of ending up on a visa blacklist – mean Western scholars often shy away from sensitive topics like 1989.

As Tiananmen's victims such as Zhang Xianling and Bao Tong age and die, we risk losing the people's history of 1989. The memory of what happened now resides behind locked doors and under police guard, in fractious communities of squabbling exiles, on the dusty shelves of university libraries and – for now at least – in the annual vigils held in Hong Kong. My aim was to try to fill some of those gaps, however imperfectly, before it was too late. Just four years later, it may already be too late.

Tiananmen matters, and to China's leaders it matters enough to mobilise the machinery of state to snuff out the tiniest commemoration. At the same time, not knowing also matters. Enforced ignorance has its own cost, best summed up in the words of one eloquent Chinese student, who attended a talk I gave at a US university. Addressing the room, she said: "I spent 18 years of my life in China and I realise now that I know nothing about my own country's history. I went to the best schools, the most well-regulated schools. And I know absolutely nothing about anything." ⊗

Louisa Lim is an award-winning journalist who reported from China for NPR and the BBC. She is the author of The People's Republic of Amnesia: Tiananmen Revisited (2014)

CREDIT:Kin Cheung/Rex

Who controls the past controls the future...

47(01): 11/13 I DOI: 10.1177/0306422018770095

Rewriting history is a global trend as governments seek to persuade people to believe their versions of events, says **Sally Gimson**

"**IF THE PARTY** could thrust its hand into the past and say of this or that event 'it never happened' – that, surely, was more terrifying than mere torture and death?" This was George Orwell, 70 years ago in his novel Nineteen Eighty-Four.

What Orwell feared is happening now. Authoritarian governments in all corners of the world are trying to construct their own version of the past, passing laws that make their versions of history the only ones allowed – and in some cases locking up historians who challenge them.

Governments in eastern Europe and Russia let go of the historical narrative for a while and allowed history to be written by individuals, civil society groups and others. For a short time after the fall of the Berlin Wall, they followed the example of countries such as Germany, which has spent much of the last 70 years coming to terms with its Nazi past.

But in the past year alone, we have seen historians sacked from museums and cultural boards in Poland, archives closed down in Hungary and Western funders of historical and civil society groups, such as George Soros, potentially barred from their home countries. In Russia, Turkey and Iran, there have been recent cases of historians detained or locked up.

Yury Dmitriev is a historian from the west of Russia, on the Finnish border. He made it his life's work to identify the people executed on Joseph Stalin's orders and buried in mass graves in the woods around his home in Sandarmokh. He has been so successful that 90% of the people murdered have now been identified. His work has been part of a project – led by a group, aptly called Memorial – which seeks to make sure that the past is remembered everywhere in Russia.

But the Russian authorities have decided they want to bury that bloody history and Memorial and Dmitriev with it. The official claim now backed up by bogus historical "evidence" is that the bodies which litter the woods are Russian prisoners of war, shot by the Finns. Dmitriev was prosecuted on trumped-up child pornography charges – of which he was cleared – and is now being detained for "assessment" on psychiatric grounds.

John Crowfoot, a British translator who has been gathering support for Dmitriev, told Index the persecution was part of →

Jan Kubik, professor of Slavonic and East European Studies at London's UCL, is not surprised about the return of authoritarianism in Russia and the persecution of historians. But he is particularly distressed about the populist nationalism emerging in Poland and Hungary.

"You have pretty remarkable change in both Hungary and Poland with the rise of right-wing populist governments. In both cases they explicitly announced some time ago that they were going to produce valid memories, valid historical knowledge, that will be of a specific ideological bent," he said. "... They will be cherry-picking those elements from the past that show those histories of those nations in the best possible light."

Kubik details other ways the Polish government is attempting to control history (see p35). For instance, the director of the Museum of the Second World War in Gdansk, Paweł Machcewicz, was sacked soon after its opening because the government did not consider the museum to be patriotic enough. It was revolutionary in its concept. It detailed not just Polish suffering but also the suffering of civilian populations throughout the world.

"It's true every government tries to participate in any subject on any topic, including the past, including the way history should be taught, including the way history should be presented in various visual displays and performances and so on," he said. "The key question is to what degree the government and the governmental vision is dominant; to what degree does the government make an effort to limit other voices and try to make its own voice exclusive, or at least dominant?"

Peter Mandler, who was until last year president of the UK's Royal Historical Society, told Index that authoritarian regimes always want to have control over the past and to control the narrative.

In India, too, Mandler said, history was being rewritten to favour the Hindu nationalist government. He cites the case of

→ a nationalist push by the government to reassert Russian greatness.

"Partly they want to refer to a great Soviet past. One of the aspects of that is the defeat of Germany and Stalin as the great leader, not a monster or a war criminal," he said.

US-based academic Wendy Doniger. Her book, Hindus: an Alternative History, was withdrawn from circulation and pulped by Penguin India after pressure from the Indian government, which considered it too favourable to Muslims.

And the list of countries dipping into authoritarianism and, by doing so, attempting to control the past goes on.

In Bangladesh, a new digital security law was proposed this year that would criminalise anyone spreading "negative propaganda" about the 1971 Liberation War or the assassinated founder of the Bangladesh nation, Sheikh Mujibur Rahman, the father of the current prime minister.

In Mexico, the army long denied responsibility for the Tlatelolco student massacre of 1968. And the government tried to deny culpability for the shooting of 41 students in 2014 who were on their way to commemorate the massacre. The government called its version of events the "historic truth".

And then there is Turkey, where about 50,000 people have been thrown into jail since the failed coup in July 2016. Although there are no specific figures for historians, academics are fleeing the country, and some 698 have applied to the New York-based Scholars at Risk to be moved abroad.

Andrew Finkel, one of the founders of the Turkish independent journalism platform P24, told Index: "It is very difficult to cross the lines of official history, although those lines are not constant. After early years of denouncing their Ottoman past, the current generation now embraces it, even at the expense of the once veneration of the founder of the republic, Mustafa Kemal Ataturk."

The fear is that, in some countries, the triumph of liberal democracy – of a way of seeing the world which allowed for multiple narratives of history – was short-lived.

And there are fears that liberal democracy is faltering even in the USA and Europe, with the new patriotism of Donald Trump and the rise of European nationalism.

Steven Levitsky, co-author of the recent book How Democracies Die, told Index that the defenders of democracy are weaker than before, and that may be why countries feel emboldened to rewrite history.

"I do think that the weakening and delegitimising of American democracy will weaken the protection of intellectuals and journalists elsewhere. The US and Europe remain important promoters of civil and human rights globally, so as they weaken and lose prestige, so to an extent does the cause of human rights. And with the US government praising and embracing nationalist autocrats, it gets worse."

Antoon de Baets, professor of history, ethics and human rights at the University of Groningen, and head of the Network of Concerned Historians, which maps the per-

Shoot the historians when you fear their history – this is what some regimes have done throughout the centuries

secution of historians across the world, is a little more upbeat. He said regimes have always sought to censor historians, but that history always won in the end.

"Shoot the historians when you fear their history – this is what some regimes have done throughout the centuries," he said.

"Lamentably, the present age is no exception; it even has the worst record. In myriad ways, the outcome of the historian's work can damage those happening to hold power and, therefore, history is always potentially threatening. History producers are fragile but in the end, and with some luck, their views may survive the regimes that killed or censored them." ⊗

Sally Gimson is a regular contributor to Index on Censorship, based in London

CREDIT: Antonio Bat/Rex

Another country

47(01): 14/18 | DOI: 10.1177/0306422018770097

This year marks 100 years since the creation of Yugoslavia. But don't expect celebrations or parades in the nations that went by this name. We don't talk about it, says **Luka Ostojić**

IN 1918, AFTER the dissolution of the Austro-Hungarian Empire, Serbs, Croats and Slovenes formed the Kingdom of Yugoslavia, creating a country that would exist for the majority of the 20th century.

In Croatia in 2018, however, there are no visible traces of this union and no formal commemorations or anniversaries of the Yugoslavian centenary. It is as though it has been wiped from history.

The reasons for this are two-fold: first, the name "Yugoslavia" has remained strongly linked to the Socialist Federal Republic of Yugoslavia, the communist state established in 1945 and dissolved in 1992. Second, in the Croatian national state it is not common to commemorate or celebrate anything concerning the Yugoslavian federation.

That detail marks Croatia's uneasy relationship with its recent history, which is mostly fixated on the events of World War II (which ended with the formation of the new Socialist Federal Republic of Yugoslavia) and the Yugoslav Wars in the 1990s (during which Yugoslavia was dissolved and the Republic of Croatia was established).

Both these periods are linked to the dialectics between nationalism and internationalism on the one hand and between fascism and anti-fascism on the other.

Croatia's nationalistic historic revisionism is a symptom of the current political vacuum: the state has had five different governments in the past 10 years, but none of them managed to implement a clear and efficient policy concerning the growing economic crisis.

Without a systematic response to social and economic issues, it is much easier to revert to old historical debates and national mythologies. This revisionism resembles the policy of the 1990s and we are seeing the same signs again.

Changes to street names and attempts to adapt the school system to reflect a particular way of seeing Croatian history are still happening. The Zagreb city government recently changed the name of Marshall Tito Square to Republic of Croatia Square. And in January 2015, the Croatian government announced a much-needed reform of the education system.

However, instead of discussing methodology, the past three years have become a battlefield between politicians, educators and activists over the education content, with the subject of history being particularly significant.

"The initial idea was to introduce a modern method of teaching by encouraging pupils to solely explore historical sources and to recognise history as a part of their everyday life. However, right-wing critics claimed that this programme didn't teach enough national history in a proper way," said Branimir Janković, a historian and researcher of 20th century Yugoslavia.

Attempts to adapt the school system to reflect a particular way of seeing Croatian history are still happening

The educational reforms are still being discussed.

In 1941, Axis powers established the Independent State of Croatia (Nezavisna država Hrvatska), the fascist puppet-state run by the nationalistic Ustasha regime, responsible for the killings of Serbs, Romas, Jews and political opponents.

However, from the outset, NDH was opposed by pan-Yugoslav, anti-fascist partisan guerilla groups. Eventually, partisans managed to defeat NDH, establish control over its territory and form a new Yugoslav state in 1945. Unlike other communist states in central and eastern Europe, it was not a part of the Soviet Union.

Janković explained how Yugoslavia constructed its identity using anti-fascist history: "In order to join together conflicted nations, the new regime introduced →

OPPOSITE: Croatian soldiers at the monument of former concentration camp Jasenovac during the commemoration for people killed during World War II

→ 'brotherhood and unity' as a key concept of the new political identity. It narrated that all Yugoslavian nations were equally leading an indisputable fight against fascism and were now joined in a solid federation. That concept included all nations, but excluded anyone not fighting on the 'right' side. It also prohibited any revision or criticism of the partisan movement."

So, during the political and economic turmoil in the 1980s, historic revisionism became a prominent part of strong national uprisings that led to the Yugoslav civil war.

During the war in the 1990s, Croatian territory was under attack by the Serbian national army and the still existing Yugoslavian National Army (JNA), which fostered nationalist, anti-Serbian and anti-Yugoslavian sentiments in Croatia. In that setting, the governing right-wing party, the Croatian Democratic Union (HDZ), decided to revise World War II history. Yugoslavian history, with an emphasis on partisan battles, was not suited to the new nationalist ideology so a new (hi)story with more focus on the Croatian nation and its urge for independence was tailored.

He managed to revive and normalise the extreme nationalistic historic revisionism

As Janković said, "HDZ decided to promote a myth of the longed-for independent national state so there was little choice but to revert to the fascist NDH, to present it as a symbol of the historic national aspiration." So the right-wing invoked NDH symbols and history while trying to ignore its fascist side.

The finest example is Jasenovac, the largest Ustasha concentration camp in Croatia, a national tragedy so manipulated that it has become a tragi-comedy. During communism, it was officially established that 700,000 people were killed in the camp. During the

1990s the new government claimed it was "just" a couple of thousand, with some politicians even suggesting that Jasenovac was a mere labour camp, with no casualties until communists turned it into a death camp. It was a clear example of the HDZ's approach. President Franjo Tuđman was cautious not to openly justify fascism, but he encouraged cleansing the NDH of its bad past and putting the label of "fascism" on new enemies. The last scientifically verified research on the Jasenovac Memorial Site has established the identities of 83,145 victims, although a final death count has yet to be established and it is not likely that this issue will ever be resolved.

The other example of historical revisionism is a paramilitary unit, the Croatian Liberating Forces (Hrvatske oslobodilačke snage, HOS), which during the 1990s openly used Ustasha symbols and praised its traditions and radical ideology.

"President Tuđman knew that every soldier was needed so he tolerated this, even though HOS soldiers were acting on their own, not following army orders," said Janković. "However, Tuđman concluded that this could harm Croatia's international reputation so, around 1992, he integrated HOS into the Croatian Army."

After the war, both HOS and the Croatian Army were uncritically praised, with an uncanny resemblance of the prior communist regime's reluctance to openly discuss the crimes committed by partisans.

Thus, in the 1990s, this revision of history was made official and implemented in schools, media, public spheres and spaces. Serbian and Yugoslavian public personas were banished from school textbooks and street names were changed with more "suitable" people taking their place. For example, the Nobel-winning Yugoslavian writer Ivo Andrić disappeared from the literature curriculum and the Ustasha writer Mile Budak appeared instead.

Fewer history textbook pages were devoted to the anti-fascist resistance and more

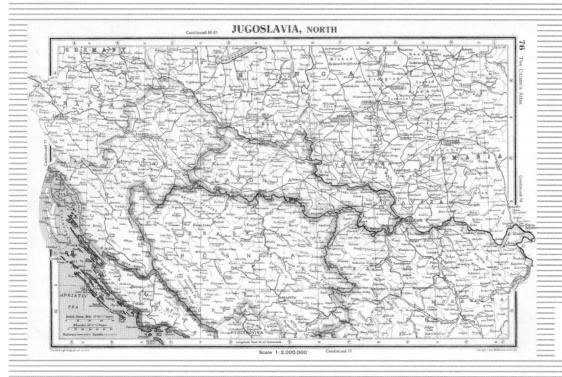

LEFT: A map of Yugoslavia

pages were devoted to NDH, with scarce reference to its fascist allies. Modernist and brutalist monuments and skyscrapers built during socialism were either destroyed or left to rot. The intention of this process was to eradicate the non-nationalist legacy of the prior 50 years and to erase the collective memory.

On the other side, with Croatia entering negotiations to become a member of the European Union in 2000, all ruling political parties consensually stopped flirting with the legacy of the fascist NDH in order to present Croatia as a modern, civic and moderate state. So, while Croatia was on its transition "upwards" (from socialism to capitalism, from Balkans to EU), mainstream historic revisionism of any kind became far less common.

That changed in 2013 for several reasons: Croatia entered the EU, so external controlling mechanisms had disappeared; the transition was completed, with no other specific political goal taking its place; and the economic crisis grew stronger, which quickly showed that entering the EU couldn't solve social issues. In 2013, the right-wing HDZ, which became more moderate during the 2000s, leaned back to the right. The party president, Tomislav Karamarko, introduced a new political programme with an emphasis on fighting against the Yugoslavian "totalitarian" legacy. He became first deputy prime minister in January 2016 and then started a process that bore striking similarities to the one from the 1990s.

Tamara Opačić, journalist, researcher and author of the report Historic Revisionism, Hate Speech and Violence against Serbs in 2016, explains measures introduced during Karamarko's mandate.

"He started using ideas and authoritarian methods common in 1990s, directly intervened in public media content, planned to change the education system and gave bigger powers to war veterans organisations, which were assigned for 'dirty jobs' of public obstruction. Although in 2013 Croatia passed a law prohibiting public denial, belittlement or condoning of genocide crimes, the law was never enforced in such cases." →

→ Karamarko's government also cut budgets for financing NGOs and non-profit media. Even though he stood down after only five months, he managed to revive and normalise the extreme nationalistic historic revisionism, deemed archaic since 2000.

And the exact same issues have become prominent again. In 2016, the right-wing filmmaker Jakov Sedlar directed a documentary film, Jasenovac – The Truth, using

The number of cases of hate speech and violence against Serbs in 2016 is higher than in 2013

falsified documents to claim that Jasenovac wasn't a concentration camp until partisans arrived. The film was heavily criticised by historians, human rights organisations and domestic and European media (such as Frankfurter Rundschau), but Sedlar was awarded the Zagreb City Award for his film. In 2017, HOS veterans erected a memorial board in Jasenovac, causing an outrage among human rights organisations. Karamarko's successor, Andrej Plenković, a more moderate right-wing politician, failed to tackle this issue. He negotiated with veterans and tried to persuade them into taking the board down. Plenković's final resolution was to move the board to the nearby village, Novska, and establish the Committee for Confrontation with Consequences of Undemocratic Regimes. Opačić called this committee "a travesty", noting that they did absolutely nothing, while adding that "it is maybe even better that way because most post-communist countries used these committees solely to equalise fascism and communism".

Finally, there is an ever-present glorification of the 1990s, with the International Criminal Court's guilty verdict of six Croatian generals, followed by General Slobodan Praljak's shocking suicide in the Hague courtroom last November, adding more fuel to the fire. In the irrational aftermath of these dramatic events, Plenković became the first head of an EU government to support convicted war criminals, telling the Croatian news agency Hina that the ICC's verdict was "a deep moral injustice towards six Croats from Bosnia and the Croatian people".

While the historic revisionism during the 1990s could be understood as a construction of the new national state mythology, it is less clear why an almost identical revisionism is repeating itself now.

Croatia has its own independent state, there are no more Serbian and communist foes, so "heroic tales" of the past seem redundant.

However, the social crisis grows and the political stalemate continues as none of the political parties seems to have an answer to striking economical issues. Without a clear policy or anyone to directly blame, this sort of revisionism seems like a nostalgia for times when enemies could be easily identified, confronted and defeated.

And we don't need to read dystopian novels or thoroughly study history books to know that such a high demand for enemies is usually followed very quickly with a supply. So, to prevent dreadful consequences of this historic revisionism, it is necessary to immediately revise the status quo politics.

Opačić's report shows that historic revisionism is followed by growing violence against minorities: the number of cases of hate speech and violence against Serbs in 2016 is higher than in 2013, with the situation allegedly even worse in 2017.

If there is one thing we can definitely learn from our recent history, it is a fact that historic revisionism doesn't reveal much about history but strongly warns us about our future. ⊗

Luka Ostojić is a Croatian journalist, based in Zagreb. He is editor-in-chief of the literary website Booksa.hr

No comfort in the truth

47(01): 19/21 I DOI: 10.1177/0306422018770099

The issue of World War II "comfort women" is back in the news as Japan refuses to revise a 2015 agreement with South Korea. What's behind the resistance, asks **Annemarie Luck**

ONE MORNING IN January 1992, long before the #MeToo movement was even an idea, a group of South Korean women gathered outside the Japanese embassy in Seoul, shouting things such as "apologise" and "shame on you". It had taken them more than 40 years to break their silence and stand up against the sexual slavery they had endured as Japan's so-called comfort women before and during World War II. Twenty-six years later, a handful of the surviving victims, along with their supporters, still gather every week at the same spot for the "Wednesday protest". And they are still waiting for a sincere official apology and acknowledgement of any legal wrongdoing.

"In a way, these women could be thought of as the original pioneers of the movement against sexual abuse and harassment that's spreading throughout the world right now," said Ho-Cheol Jeong, team leader of the International Outreach Team at the House of Sharing, which is located in Gwangju, a city on the outskirts of Seoul, and serves as a shelter for surviving victims.

"Kim Hak-Sun was the first to give testimony during a press conference in 1991. She was the one who brought the issue to light."

Inspired by her example, many more women – not only from South Korea but also from the Philippines, China, Taiwan, Malaysia, Burma, East Timor, Indonesia, the Netherlands and Japan – have come forward, giving detailed accounts of the horrific conditions and brutality they suffered between 1932 and 1945. The total number of victims is unclear, but estimates range between 80,000 and 200,000. Many of the women, often in their teens, were kidnapped or recruited with false promises of employment. They were taken to "comfort stations" set up around Asia by the Japanese military and forced to work as prostitutes, servicing many men every day.

In her testimony, Kim Hak-Sun stated: "Around 300 soldiers could take a break from duty once every three days. Each woman had to serve an average of three to four soldiers on regular days, and seven to eight soldiers after battles." The women endured not only painful sexually transmitted diseases but also forced abortions. Many died. And once the war ended, they were simply abandoned to their own devices – often not even in their home countries – and lived under a weight of shame and stigmatisation.

As of 2016, 239 women had registered with the South Korean government as →

→ victims of Japanese military sexual slavery. Nine of them, now aged between 88 and 102, live at the House of Sharing. The "grandmothers", as Ho-Cheol Jeong calls them, are starting to lose their memories and some suffer from dementia, so they are no longer able to give interviews and tell their stories. Speaking on their behalf, Ho-Cheol explains that they are still fighting to regain their dignity. "Their first request is for the Japanese government to recognise that this was a war crime and for it not to be repeated. They continue to ask for a formal apology to teach the next generation about what happened. These women are living proof of history, but the Japanese government is just waiting for the old victims to pass away because they think the issue will then disappear."

So where does the Japanese government stand on the issue? On the surface, it could be argued that they have apologised numerous times and offered compensation. But in the eyes of the victims and their advocates, their apology is half-hearted, calibrated to avoid legal responsibility and constantly undermined by conservatives' denials and denunciations. Also, the government has backtracked and broken promises, going so far as to delete references to comfort women from school textbooks.

"The government did admit to coercively recruiting comfort women in the 1993 Kono Statement and promised to atone for this and to educate the Japanese about this sordid system of sexual slavery," said Jeff Kingston, director of Asian studies at Temple University, Japan. "But this latter pledge has been broken. Twenty years ago, all of Japan's mainstream secondary school textbooks covered the comfort women, and now none of them do, at Prime Minister Shinzo Abe's behest."

Kingston said that, under Abe, a more nationalist narrative of imperial Japan has become mainstream.

"All nations beautify their history, but few have backtracked so far, so fast, from a forthright reckoning as Japan since the mid-1990s," he said. "This nationalist backlash, under the banner of revisionism, has been led by Abe, the backslider-in-chief, who is committed to rehabilitating Japan's colonial and wartime history to posthumously honour his grandfather, former PM Kishi Nobusuke – a class-A war crimes suspect for his role in recruiting slave labour in Manchuria, and signing the order to attack Pearl Harbor. Revisionists deny, downplay and shift responsibility for misdeeds and atrocities, while also arguing 'everyone else did the same things, so why pick on us?'."

One result of this is South Korea recently coming forward to challenge the 2015 agreement it reached with Japan, in which Japan offered one billion yen ($9 million) to support comfort women. In late 2017, the minister of foreign affairs of South Korea, Kang Kyung-wha, called for a reconsideration of the agreement, saying that it failed to meet the needs of victims.

But Japan's minster of foreign affairs, Taro Kono, hit back, releasing a statement this January: "The Japan-South Korea agreement is an agreement between the two governments, and one that has been highly appreciated by international society. If the South Korean government … tried to revise the agreement that is already being implemented, that would make Japan's ties with South Korea unmanageable and it would be unacceptable."

Kingston, however, points out the agreement's major flaws: "The 2015 agreement is a diplomatic deceit that never had any legitimacy because it sidelined the comfort women from the process and negotiations were conducted secretly, as if this was a sensitive arms deal rather than an effort to address a profound violation of human rights. It doesn't meet global standards for addressing violence against women in war and lacks a victim-centred approach. It is an exceptionally one-sided agreement – one that, for Japan, is too good to be true."

Yuki Tanaka, a historian and the author of Japan's Comfort Women, agreed, saying: "Abe effectively tried to buy the complete silence of South Korea on the comfort women issue. He basically said, 'We'll give you one billion yen so you'll shut up'."

When asked why he thinks Japan has been so reluctant to admit responsibility on the issue of comfort women, Tanaka has an insightful viewpoint. He goes into some detail explaining how, when Japan surrendered to the USA at the end of World War II, they made a deal. "It's what I call the US-Japan conspiracy," he said.

According to Tanaka, it was agreed that the USA would keep former Emperor Hirohito's reputation intact, masking his war crimes by saying he had been taken advantage of by "a small group of war mongrels". In return, Japan would downplay the USA's

crime against humanity committed when they dropped the atomic bombs on Hiroshima and Nagasaki.

"So the majority of Japanese people not only failed to form a clear idea about their nation's war responsibility, but also came to see themselves as victims of war rather than perpetrators. This mentality is what I call the sense of victimhood without identifying victimisers … As a result, the morality of the Japanese people is completely wrong. They don't pursue justice."

Tanaka takes his theory one step further and cites Japan's patriarchal societal system as a contributing factor. "Underneath the comfort women issue, the 'misogynistic masculinity' of Japanese men, and the way they treat women, is the problem," he said. "The number of female parliamentarians in the lower house of the Diet is only 39 out of 480. Such statistics make it almost unsurprising that 'comfort-women bashing' is rife in the Diet."

On top of this, while women around the world are becoming increasingly vocal about the sexual harassment and abuse they've suffered at the hands of men, Japanese women

Each woman had to serve an average of three to four soldiers on regular days, and seven to eight soldiers after battles

are still largely silent on the matter.

"Sexual exploitation is a big issue in Japan, but we have to change not only the Japanese men's way of thinking but also the women's ideas. If we want to change or improve the issue of the comfort women, we have to change Japanese society as a whole," said Tanaka. ⊗

Annemarie Luck is based in Tokyo, Japan, and is the editor-in-chief of Tokyo Weekender magazine

OPPOSITE: Girl and grandmother statues representing comfort women at the weekly rally in front of the Japanese Embassy in Seoul, South Korea, 27 December 2017

Unleashing the past

47(01): 22/25 | DOI: 10.1177/0306422018770100

A century after an independent Armenia was born, **Kaya Genç** reports on how Ottoman Armenian history is discussed in Turkey today

INDEXONCENSORSHIP.ORG

LEFT: A traditional Ottoman band protest the approval of a resolution by Germany's parliament to call the 1915 massacre of Armenians a "genocide", Istanbul 2016

BOOKS ABOUT OTTOMAN Armenians are increasingly popular in Turkey. Hitherto locked archives have become accessible for research over the last decade, and texts that view the killings of Ottoman Armenians in the early 20th century from dramatically different perspectives are sold largely without restrictions. But while historical research into some subjects has been opened up in Turkey, interrogating the past is, by and large, problematic.

The word "genocide", when applied to the expulsion and killing of Armenians that took place between 1915 and 1917, remains contested, as do the numbers of those who died.

Meanwhile, a new bill, passed by Turkey's constitutional committee on 21 July 2017, has even gone so far as banning any mention of this episode by parliamentarians. Those who talk of it in parliament can now have deductions made from their →

→ salaries and can be barred from attending parliamentary sessions.

This year is a particularly significant year for Turkey-Armenia ties. A century ago, in 1918, Armenians formed a sovereign state for the first time since 1375. The First Republic of Armenia, as it is now known, took land away from the Ottoman Empire and was home to more than one million people. It lasted for just a few years. In 1922, Armenia was incorporated into the former Soviet Union and it lost independence until 1991. In April, Turkey's president, Recep Tayyip Erdogan, will likely send a message to Turkish Armenians to "respectfully commemorate the Ottoman Armenians who died under the tough conditions of World War I and offer my condolences to their grandchildren", as he has been doing since 2014.

Armenians and governments of more than 29 countries label the deaths of Armenians during this period as genocide. The Turkish state calls it *tehcir*, or forced displacement. This has resulted in a lot of animosity between both sides. In the past, many Armenian nationalists portrayed Ottoman Turks as culpable and barbaric, while Turkish nationalists have accused Armenians of lying

Turkish censors reacted swiftly to this attempt at uncovering a hidden history

about their extermination, some saying they deserved being massacred because of their disloyalty to the Ottoman Empire. (Armenians were accused of sympathising with invading Russian forces during the war when Turkey was allied with Germany.)

This polarisation was challenged by the intellectual Hrant Dink. In columns for Agos, the newspaper he edited for years – the only one published in both Turkish and Armenian at the time – he pointed to a third, humanistic way of dealing with past atrocities.

"I challenge the accepted version of history because I do not write about things in black and white. People here are used to black and white; that's why they are astonished that there are other shades, too," he said.

While Dink used the word "genocide", he acknowledged that it was politically loaded and called for conciliation between the two sides, effectively rewriting the history of Turkish-Armenian animosities.

"In the past, Armenians have trusted the West to save them from the oppression they suffered at the hands of Ottoman officials," Dink said in 2006. "But they were mistaken. Foreigners came, made their own calculations and left brothers and sisters at each other's throats."

Dink wanted Turks and Armenians to come together to figure out their histories, to ask why, how and what, rather than point fingers.

His willingness to bridge two cultures was brutally punished in January 2007, when a 17-year-old nationalist shot him in the back in broad daylight in central Istanbul.

Dink's assassination and the outrage it produced sparked a massive interest in the Armenian question among Turkish readers.

In 2010, Tuba Çandar, a seasoned journalist and editor, wrote his biography, Hrant, a 700-page tome that became a bestseller.

"We can say that it is easier for historians and journalists to write about the Armenian issue in today's Turkey," Çandar told Index. "Turkish intellectuals began discussing the Armenian issue in the second half of the 1990s. The process began with Vahakn Dadrian's The History of the Armenian Genocide, a book published by Belge Publishing."

Turkish censors reacted swiftly to this attempt at uncovering a hidden history. Dadrian's book was confiscated, Belge Publishing was bombed and the publisher was put on trial. But the book reached readers through pirated editions and broke a Turkish taboo.

"The two-decades-long struggle to openly discuss the issue, and the murder of Hrant Dink, made the Armenian genocide discussable among intellectuals in Turkey," Çandar said. She considers Dink's funeral in Istanbul in 2007 – attended by 250,000 people who cried "We are all Armenians, we are all Hrant!" – as a watershed moment. "The word 'Armenian' had been used pejoratively in Turkey until Dink's murder. But not since."

This new atmosphere was strengthened in 2008 by a petition, signed by 30,000 people, which apologised for the treatment of Ottoman Armenians. The international Hrant Dink Association was formed and numerous high-profile intellectuals including Noam Chomsky and Naomi Klein visited Istanbul to deliver annual Dink lectures.

In their hands, Dink's legacy of reconsidering history and its links to politics survived.

Despite all public marches being banned in Turkey in the aftermath of the attempted July 2016 coup, on 19 January this year, I walked with thousands in central Istanbul to commemorate the 11th anniversary of Dink's assassination. The government did nothing to stop the march.

But Çandar is pessimistic about the future. She thinks the mass purges of Turkish scholars in the aftermath of the 2016 coup attempt may result in the return of the official state line about the Armenian issue – that Armenians had it coming – and the new parliamentary bill is another sign that the recent openness about Armenia might be nearing an end. "The government now views Kurds, rather than Armenians, as the inner threat, but that does not mean the Armenian issue will be freely debated in public in the future," she said.

Freedoms in the Turkish publishing world remain fragile. When, in 2007, an Istanbul publisher released a Turkish version of Robert Fisk's The Great War for Civilisation: The Conquest of the Middle East, there were fears of prosecution under Article 301 of the Turkish penal code that made "insulting Turkishness" a crime. These fears proved unfounded. Still, publishers feel they need to be careful about the Armenian issue, and Ragıp Zarakolu, a writer, publisher and activist who has been targeted in Turkey for publishing books on minority and human rights, is aware of the remaining restrictions.

"Nowadays, it is easier to study and publish on the issue," he told Index. "Article

Still publishers feel they need to be careful about the Armenian issue

301 is no longer used, but it remains in the penal code and is the major legal threat on the issue."

In 1987, Zarakolu won a court case and successfully defended his right to put out a book on Ottoman Armenians. His win paved the way for other books on the subject.

"With Belge Publishing, we expanded the limits of the debate about the Armenian genocide through civil disobedience," he said. The publisher bypassed bans by distributing books in the form of photocopies and within a small but influential readership Belge books reached their audience.

"We were influential in turning taboos into subjects that the public could analyse and discuss," Zarakolu added. "But we paid the price of that with bans and trials."

Because of social pressures, Zarakolu believes books that explore the issue bravely sometimes can't find space in bookstores.

"In the 1990s, young people had little knowledge about the issue. Nowadays, they are largely under the influence of the official narrative about heinous Armenians betraying the nation. But among intellectuals, refusal to acknowledge the issue is no longer an option." ⊗

Kaya Genç is a contributing editor to Index on Censorship, based in Istanbul

47(01): 26/27 | DOI: 10.1177/0306422018770102

Rowson

MARTIN ROWSON is a cartoonist for The Guardian and the author of various books, including Coalition Book (2014), a collection of cartoons about the UK's years under a coalition government

twitter@pacobaca

CREDIT: Paco Baca/Cartoon Movement

Tracing a not too dissident past

47(01): 28/30 I DOI: 10.1177/0306422018770103

After 59 years of rule by the Castro family, Cuba is getting ready for a presidential transition. Can an online project accurately portray the country's rebellious history, asks **Irene Caselli**

BEING LABELLED AS a rebel in Cuba can come at a heavy price. Over the years, dissidents have been imprisoned, persecuted and distanced from public life. And yet the country was effectively founded by those who overthrew the system and is still run by revolutionaries.

As Raúl Castro gets ready to step down as Cuba's president on 19 April, after nearly six decades of Castro rule, two artists based in Havana are keen to highlight Cuba's history, and particularly its untold tales.

"All the heroes of Cuba's history, even Hatuey [an indigenous chief], were dissidents

EL CASTRO

926-2016

at one point in time," Cuban artist Luis Manuel Otero Alcántara told Index.

"But here in Cuba it is stigmatised. It is paired with negative words such as *gusano* (worm) or mercenary. It is a simple word, but if you use it, or if the government attributes it to you, people will distance themselves because they are afraid they will also be deemed dissidents."

Otero and his partner, art curator Yanelys Nuñez Leyva, operate the Cuban Museum of Dissidence, a website that lists all those who stood up against the government during the history of the Caribbean island. The online art project challenges the negative connotations of the word, taking Cuba's history as proof of its positive contributions.

The website's banner features images of late president Fidel Castro; Oswaldo Payá, a Catholic political activist who opposed the regime for more than two decades; 19th century national hero José Martí; and Hatuey, an indigenous Taíno chief who fled from the island of Hispaniola to warn the people of

Cuba about the Spanish invaders in 1511. They remind visitors that Fidel Castro, together with his brother Raúl and Argentine revolutionary Ernesto "Che" Guevara, led an armed revolt against the US-backed regime of Fulgencio Batista, which culminated in Batista's escape in 1959 and the establishment of a socialist regime.

"We tell the government: 'You were once dissidents, you should allow dissidence'," said Otero. "And we tell dissidents: 'Careful, because one day you may end up in power and you may clamp down on dissidents, too'."

But this message, and their work, has not been well-received by everyone. When the project was launched in 2016, it quickly caused the couple trouble. Nuñez worked as a staff writer at Revolución y Cultura, a magazine published by Cuba's Ministry of Culture. She believes she was fired because of her involvement with the museum. Index contacted magazine editor Luisa Campuzano to confirm whether or not this was true, but received no response.

Otero said the museum website was now blocked in Cuba and they relied on Facebook and other social networks to post information related to the project. The museum is not the couple's only provocative work – this January, they created an installation

We tell the government: you were once dissidents, you should allow dissidence

featuring a fictional version of Fidel Castro's last will after Otero said the late president came to him in a dream, asking the people for forgiveness – but it is the one that has caused them the most trouble. Otero relates how he was detained twice in 2017 and has been followed and threatened on several occasions. He stresses that he and Nuñez are not aligned with any opposition groups. →

CREDIT: Rodrigo Abd/Rex

ABOVE: The different faces of Fidel Castro on display in an art gallery, Cuba

→ On the contrary, they try to present historical information without judgment. This is quite a challenge in Cuba, where resources on contemporary history are not always reliable.

"Information regarding the history of contemporary dissidence in Cuba exists, but it's scattered," said Nuñez.

For example, Cuba's government-curated version of Wikipedia, EcuRed, gives negative opinions of contemporary critics.

Blogger Yoani Sánchez, who is renowned worldwide for her critical view of the government, is described as a "cyber mercenary" in the EcuRed entry, while Oswaldo Payá, the late political activist, is said to have been a "Cuban counter-revolutionary linked to the United States".

To build the museum, its creators got together with friends and historians to gather as much information as possible, including using Wikipedia as a source of information for many of the profiles they put together. While they are keen to stress that they are not historians, they aim to create a thought-provoking project that challenges the idea of how history is constructed.

Describing how the subject is taught in Cuban schools, Nuñez said: "It is a chronological recounting of deeds and dates." But Otero went further: "Education is not free in Cuba," he said. "What is free is indoctrination. You can never question history in school, because if you ask questions you get kicked out."

With the presidential transition coming up, will dissidents have a say in Cuba's new political phase, one deemed to be of greater openness? Judging from the 2017 municipal elections, the chances are low.

A platform known as Otro18 ("Another 18", a reference to the electoral year) said it had tried to register about 170 opposition candidates for the 2017 elections, but none got on the ballot.

And in an apparently leaked video, First Vice President Miguel Díaz Canel, the man widely expected to be the next president, indicated that he was in favour of shutting down the Miami-based OnCuba website – which fosters communication between Cuba and the USA – calling it "very aggressive against the revolution".

"Let the scandal ensue. Let them say we censure, it's fine. Everyone censors," he said in the Miami Herald.

Otero believes that, despite the changes to come, there will still be a need for resistance.

"Right now I am afraid that all this change is going to be a sham. Social networks, websites, everything is monitored," he said. "Dissidence is necessary." ⊗

Luis Manuel Otero Alcántara and *Yanelys Nuñez Leyva, as part of The Museum of Dissidence, have been shortlisted for the Index on Censorship 2018 Freedom of Expression Awards*

Irene Caselli is an Index contributing editor who has spent the last decade reporting from Latin America

Lessons in bias

47(01): 31/34 I DOI: 10.1177/0306422018770109

History is under attack. It is being manipulated, used and abused by national leaders around the world. Here we interview five leading historians about what happens when history becomes a weapon

A WAR ON FACTS

RACHAEL JOLLEY interviews MARGARET MACMILLAN on German myth making about World War I

Authoritarian leaders, and others, have often taken history seriously, because if they control history, they control their own legitimacy, said Canadian historian Margaret MacMillan.

She points to how the first Chinese emperor, in 221BC, called in all the history books and burnt them, then wrote his own version.

History, the Oxford University professor said, can have a lot of power. "The thing about history is, if people only know one version then it seems to validate the people in power," adding that "the great thing about history is it can open up your mind, and you can say we didn't have to come down this path".

MacMillan, who writes extensively on World War I, said there were many examples of governments trying to control the historical record. "The German foreign office had a whole unit in the 1920s that was devoted to selecting and publishing German documents leading up to the war," she said.

"Because the war was so dreadful, the question of who was responsible was a very important one. Governments tried [to establish] that it wasn't their fault, it was someone else's.

"But the Germans also thought that they hadn't really lost, and that was a myth that was propagated by certain people."

MacMillan explains that view also took root in the English-speaking countries and fed into the way the Western powers responded in the 1930s by allowing Germany leeway.

"A lot of people came to think in Britain and the United States that, yes, Germany had been unfairly treated and it should be appeased," she said. "[That] Austria should have been allowed to merge with Germany at the end of the war.

"So even with Anschluss – when Germany took over Austria in the beginning of 1938 – a lot of people in the English-speaking countries said 'well, you know, Germany was treated unfairly'."

MacMillan also spoke of the impact of national leaders using historical stories as a platform for their nationalism, and why the role of historians was so important.

"Stories have been created by creating a national history, helped to create a sense of a nation, so it is not nationalism coming first, then historians following on, it's historians."

She said: "George Orwell got it completely. History can be subversive, it can be a tool of dictators."

MacMillan feels strongly that history needs to be taught well in schools. It's important to know that when you learn about a particular event, you are not hearing everything. But it is essential that every version is based on facts.

"I guess the best you can do is encourage people to ask questions."

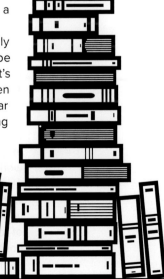

HISTORY'S BAD GUYS AREN'T SO BAD

NEIL OLIVER believes the Vikings deserve a historical makeover, writes JEMIMAH STEINFELD

When it comes to the Vikings, history has been written by the victims, not the victors – and that's equally problematic.

"The Vikings were the last people in Europe to adopt Christianity. They remained pagans for longer than anyone," Neil Oliver, the British archaeologist and presenter of hit shows including the BBC's Vikings, told Index. He explains that Christianity played an essential role in introducing writing in Europe, which made a big difference to the way history was recorded.

"They couldn't write the history that they were inflicting on others," he said. "Other people they came into contact with wrote it and, because they usually didn't like them, they portrayed them as murderous, as pagans and as villains."

As a result, the Vikings have suffered from bad PR, both at the time of their conquests and in the centuries since. How easy is it to overcome this bias? Oliver said that, fortunately, there are other sources out there, which allow historians to get a better sense of who the Vikings actually were.

"When the Vikings began penetrating Europe, they came into contact with Muslims sent in for the Caliphate... along the Danube, the Tigris, and other European areas."

While Oliver said that not all impressions were positive (Muslims would often remark on how the Vikings smelled bad and that they were disgusted by some of their customs), they did, nevertheless, write about them "quite favourably".

"And you do have the Viking sagas and they were based on oral traditions," he said, adding the caveat that these were written hundreds of years after the time, "so distance of time compromises those events".

"In context, the Vikings were almost certainly no worse than anyone," he said.

Context is, of course, key and this is something Oliver is also keen to highlight in reference to how more contemporary events, namely the EU and the internet, are viewed.

"I'm watching the present geopolitical situation and am struck by parallels between Brexit and the internet and how both are being presented."

As with the Vikings, he believes history is being cherry-picked and is shifting

MINORITY REPORT

CHARLES VAN ONSELEN tells RACHAEL JOLLEY how the past was rewritten during apartheid

"Ever since the age of the telegraph and the steam ship in the mid-19th century, the world is becoming increasingly globalised, but textbooks are written as if the nation state is the only entity and sort of offers the only levers of control in society – and this is manifestly nonsense," argues

leading South African historian Charles van Onselen.

He has an example at hand of how a nationalist political power attempted to use a historical rewrite of its country's past to manipulate public opinion. During South Africa's apartheid years, the Afrikaner-run government rewrote primary and secondary-school history books, before moving on to university textbooks a decade later. Van Onselen, a professor in the Centre for the Advancement of Scholarship

at Pretoria University, describes how it started after the election of 1948. The government used the power of a secret organisation, the Broederbond, to influence the teaching profession.

"So the first thing that happens is that the school textbooks get rewritten and this manifests itself in wide-scale rewriting of history, foregrounding Afrikaner nationals' experience and their destiny as chosen people," he said.

"Central to that is this event

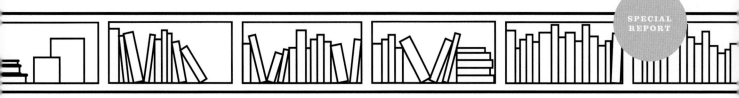

our reality of the two. Oliver discusses how both the EU and the internet were born of conflict (the idea of the EU partly coming from the Marshall Plan – a US initiative giving assistance to help rebuild western European economies after World War II – and the internet growing out of the USA's Defense Advanced Research Projects Agency, which "was a response to the launch of Sputnik" and "a great paranoia of the Soviet control of space").

"It's [the internet] portrayed now as if it was always this benign system that brings people together, but that's not what it was created as," said Oliver.

"I don't see the wartime context for the foundations of either being talked about. A fractured, splintered Europe could have bad consequences. It's not censored, it's just not there."

SEPARATE PAST

ED KEAZOR talks to WANA UDOBANG on silencing Biafra

The Nigerian Civil War, more commonly known as the Biafran War, is one of Nigeria's most defining events. But suppression of information about this conflict, which lasted from 1967 to 1970, is having unintended consequences now.

"When you put a lid on something for so many years – and it's boiling – when you finally open the lid, the steam or smoke blows everywhere and that is what is happening," said Nigerian historian Ed Keazor.

Today, Nigeria is experiencing a growth in separatist movements across the country. Some claim the deliberate silencing of the war is responsible.

"A lot of the documentation of the civil war was not contained in any academic text, particularly for younger people," he said. "People had to rely on the narratives of interested actors with their own subjective views."

An absence of documentation and spin from both the Nigerian government and the Biafran separatists led to significant censorship during the military era (1970 to 1999).

"There was certainly a 'don't talk about the war' [culture] amongst publishers," said Keazor. "And it was a psychology that continued even when there was a civilian regime in the second republic."

History was also taken off the education curriculum, which many claimed was a deliberate move by the government.

"It was felt by some that the removal of history as a whole was to prevent some unpleasant aspects in the nation's history from being highlighted."

of 1838 when they prayed and asked for God's guidance for victory over the indigenous people and Blood River [a battle], and that becomes a central organising principle for the ethnic destiny."

Van Onselen, who writes books on Afrikaner history, said: "It was laying down the political and ideological template groundwork for grand apartheid that was emerging in the 1960s, by saying you have got a separate geographical area, you have got a separate

culture, you've got a separate history and indeed you will live separately."

But, ultimately, this attempt to rewrite the nation's history was not successful, because huge swathes of the population did not believe it, he argues.

"The history textbook rewriting comes from a manifest minority with a very particular ethnic and racial agenda in a country that is manifestly multiracial, multilingual and multicultural."

Van Onselen is, however,

not a fan of how history is being taught today in South Africa. He argues that very little is taught about wider African history.

"Our archives, our libraries, our documentary collections are in an utterly disgraceful and decayed state. Nationalists in South Africa - white and black alike - give pride of place to the role of history in their 'struggle'."

"Little time and money is spent on preservation of our historical records."

ONLY A FOOL BELIEVED HE HAD FREE SPEECH

Tudor historians were at the service of their monarchs, and we live with this legacy, historian and author LUCY WORSLEY tells Index

In the scenes of my historical novels set at the Tudor court, freedom of speech was not a privilege held by many people. In fact, come to think of it, maybe only by the king's fool, or jester – a truth-telling character who I've used as a fictional device in a novel about a maid of honour arriving at the court of Henry VIII and negotiating some of the power politics she found there.

You can see exactly why Henry VIII took the trouble to control his kingship so carefully – not just through the written medium but also through things like the design of his palaces, his public appearances and even who was allowed to come into his presence. His father had seized the throne in a coup just a generation before, and everyone was used

to the upheaval of the Wars of the Roses. In a notorious piece of Tudor history rewriting, Henry VII dated the start of his reign from before the Battle of Bosworth, as if he'd been king all along, and when he won at Bosworth he was really just seizing the crown back again from the usurper Richard III – rather than Henry VII himself being the usurper.

Of course, historians today can see how Tudor historians were working for whoever was in power at the time and rewriting history to suit: just look at historian John Rous, who first praised Richard III to the skies when he was in power, then did the same for Henry VII in due course, and then blackened Richard III's name after his fall.

Tudor propaganda was remarkably effective, whether it focused on the achievements of individual monarchs, or more generally when we look at the visual branding, the palace building, the heraldry and royal devices and image-making through artists such as Holbein from the 16th century. These are people we're still talking about 500 years later:

they had excellent public relations to have ensured that their reputations have lasted half a millennium.

But there were limits to Tudor power. The other thing that gave moral certainty to the writers of the 16th century was religion, and that's something that can lead to powerful storytelling. For a novelist, the fate of Protestants under Catholic monarchs such as Mary I, or Catholics under Protestant monarchs such as Elizabeth I, instantly places characters in jeopardy. Your belief in heaven and hell and how these things might affect you personally will be yours and yours alone to a Tudor person, and not even a king or queen, however great their power, can force you to change your mind.

It's sometimes amusing to make jokes at Tudor head chopping as it all seems so safely distant. But it isn't so funny if you think of what people still do in the name of religious fundamentalism today.

Lucy Worsley is joint chief curator at the Historic Royal Palaces and a BBC presenter ⊗

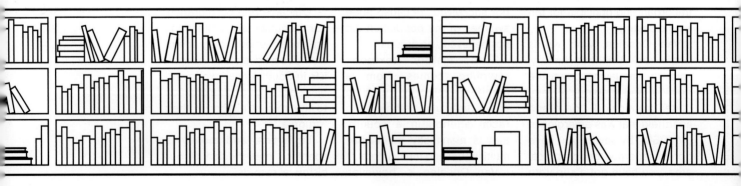

Projecting Poland and its past

47(01): 35/37 | DOI: 10.1177/0306422018770110

A museum commemorating the "Polocaust" is the next plan for Poland's history project. **Konstanty Gebert** reports on why

HAVE YOU HEARD of the Polocaust? The PR guru to Poland's ruling party leader Jarosław Kaczyński is on a mission to make sure you do.

"The Polish state does not have at its disposal an institution which would, similarly to Yad Vashem [The Holocaust museum in Israel], show the suffering which had befallen the Poles," laments Marek Kochan, PR advisor to Kaczyński of Poland's Law and Justice party.

Kochan calls this suffering "the Polocaust".

In an article published in the Warsaw daily Rzeczpospolita, Kochan argues that such a museum is necessary and can, and should, be built in one year. "We can invite Prime Minister Benjamin Netanyahu for the opening," he suggested. "The recent debate has shown that there is in Israel a deficit of knowledge about World War II, even among opinion-makers."

He refers here to Israeli reactions to the recent passing by the Polish parliament of a law which would penalise, with up to three years in jail, anyone making "allegations that the Polish state or the Polish nation were responsible or co-responsible for the Nazi crimes of the German Third Reich", among other things.

It generated outrage in Israel, where the memory of wartime betrayals committed by many Poles, alongside that of selfless help at

the risk of their lives by others, is still alive.

One of the first to react was Israeli opposition MP Yair Lapid, who tweeted: "I utterly condemn the new Polish law which attempts to deny Polish complicity in the Holocaust... There were Polish death camps and no law can ever change that."

The Polish embassy tweeted in reply: →

ABOVE: Far-right protest in Warsaw, Poland, February 2018 in favour of introducing a penalty for using the term Polish death or concentration camps

III

HOLOCAUST LAW: THE STORY SO FAR

....

• Polish-born historian Jan Gross collided with Poland's Law and Justice party (PiS) over an article he wrote in a September 2015 issue of Germany's Die Welt newspaper. In it he said Poles killed more Jews during World War II than they did Nazis. Polish Foreign Ministry spokesman Marcin Wojciechowski described it as "historically untrue, harmful and insulting to Poland". Prosecutors investigated whether Gross had broken laws prohibiting defamation of Poland and there were calls for the removal of his Order of Merit of the Republic of Poland.

• Around the time of the anniversary of the liberation of Auschwitz, on 27 January, a rumour spread that Poles weren't invited. Other rumours circulated including a claim that singing the Polish national anthem was banned, according to Bloomberg. Meanwhile, a government-appointed curator for Auschwitz said only Polish nationals should have a licence to guide visitors, to ensure the message was not anti-Polish.

• Polish Prime Minister Mateusz Morawiecki stirred the pot in February when he said that "it would not be punishable or criminal if you say there were Polish perpetrators, just like there were Jewish perpetrators". The remark was made when an Israeli journalist asked him at a conference if Poland would consider him a criminal after he reported Polish neighbours had betrayed his Jewish family to the Gestapo. Israeli Prime Minister Benjamin Netanyahu called it "outrageous".

• A campaign group close to the ruling Polish party filed charges of defamation against Argentinian newspaper Página/12 this March, the first case after the law was passed. Página/12 published an article in December 2017 about the massacre of Jews in Jedwabne in 1941, featuring an image of anti-communist Polish partisans. The Polish League Against Defamation claims confusing the image of the partisans with the issue of Jedwabne is defamatory. Since then, other media have shared the article.

Jemimah Steinfeld

→ "Your unsupportable claims show how badly Holocaust education is needed, even here in Israel." A furious Lapid, citing a grandmother allegedly "murdered in Poland by Germans and Poles", demanded an apology. None was forthcoming, and matters went downhill from there.

While the polemic still rages, the Lapid exchange provides necessary background to Kochan's seemingly extravagant proposal. The Israeli politician was entirely right in suggesting that the goal of the new law is to stifle debate about the scale of complicity of many Poles in the Holocaust (even the authorities do not deny individual cases of atrocities), and entirely and insultingly wrong in claiming the existence of "Polish death camps". Poland and the Poles had nothing to do with the decision of German-occupying authorities to build their camps on Polish soil, nor did they play any role in their operation. The fact that such an allegation can be made, many in Poland believe, is clear proof that the world ignores Polish history and Polish suffering, and needs to be educated about it.

In fact, it needs to learn that Poles, far from being responsible for the camps, were their victims (100,000 non-Jewish Poles were killed in Auschwitz alone). In all, of the six million – or 17% of the Polish population exterminated in World War II – half were Polish Jews and half were non-Jewish Poles.

But even if this is the case, does it matter?

Yes, say the advocates of this viewpoint. Once the world realises the scale of Polish suffering and heroism in World War II, it will not only stop slandering us the way Lapid did, but also realise we are a great and noble nation. Such nations deserve respect and gratitude, but also compensation: both in the political sense – our wartime allies have a duty to support us against Israeli slander, Russian threats and Ukrainian insolence (the issue of crimes against the Polish population in what is now Ukraine is another raw and sensitive issue) – and also financially. The right-wing government in power in Warsaw since 2015 says it intends to demand reparations from Germany for losses incurred in World War II, to the tune of hundreds of billions of dollars.

Arguments over the new Polish law have brought things to a boil, but wars of memory had been going on in Poland for some time.

The new Museum of the Second World War, in Gdansk, was inaugurated last year. This in itself was a victory as the minister of culture had, from the onset, announced that he considered the museum a disgrace, and wanted to dismiss its director and change the exhibition. He cited expert opinions he had commissioned, one of which complained that the museum "presents a too negative picture of the war", meaning it did not sufficiently underscore the heroism and solidarity that conflict can reveal in people. Another often-voiced complaint is that the museum "fails to present the Polish viewpoint".

The first criticism is entirely justified: the museum presents the war as an unmitigated disaster, of which Poland was the first victim, and one of the most horribly affected by it.

The second is supremely unclear, unless it implies the total rejection of the museum's underlying premise of showing the war as a universal, not only Polish, experience.

Be that as it may, the government's war on the museum has been largely successful. The director, Paweł Machcewicz, has been fired and now attempts are being made to change

the exhibition, presumably to make it more sympathetic to the Polish viewpoint. As it is copyright-protected this might prove more challenging, but a first point has been scored.

A documentary film concluding the exhibition showing post-World War II conflicts through the Cold War, the end of communism and present-day Syria has been eliminated. One of the reasons given is that it shows, in a brief sequence of a Polish opposition demonstration in the 80s, Paweł Adamowicz, then a student activist and now the opposition mayor of Gdansk, who is supremely disliked by the regime. Thus, as far as the museum is concerned, Adamowicz has become an Orwellian non-person.

But international public opinion has rightly seen the museum takeover and the new

The government's war on the museum has been largely successful

law as shameful attempts to rewrite history. Much of Polish opinion, which is critical of the government, shares this view.

With Kochan wielding considerable influence within the ruling party his Polocaust Museum might actually be built as part of the government's attempts to lash its version of history to its own agenda. The deputy minister of culture has already endorsed the idea. If it happens, this desperate attempt to paint Polish history in the national white and red only – white for innocence, red for bloodshed – is doomed to failure.

And this failure will unavoidably make it even more difficult to educate world opinion – often misinformed, disinterested and disengaged – that the all-too-real history of Polish suffering deserves a sympathetic hearing. ⊗

Konstanty Gebert is based in Warsaw and writes for Polish daily newspaper Gazeta Wyborcza

47(01): 38/39 | DOI: 10.1177/0306422018770111

Battle lines

How is the same episode of history being taught in two countries? We asked **Hannah Leung** and **Matthew Hernon** to talk to young people in China and Japan to find out what they were taught about the highly controversial Nanjing Massacre

CHINA

China marked the 80th anniversary of the Nanjing Massacre on 13 December 2017. On that day in 1937, Japanese military troops invaded Nanjing, killing an estimated 300,000 people. We asked young people in both Japan and China the same set of questions to see differences in history teaching.

MATTHEW XIA, 26

I: Did you learn about Nanjing at school?
MX: Yes, we covered the Nanjing Massacre in both middle and high school.
I: How was it referred to?
MX: It was referred to as the Nanjing Massacre. It was definitely one of the most anticipated chapters because, as students, we heard about it before and wanted to know all the details. I felt a bit daunted as it was so terrifying and involved a lot of killing.
I: Who was involved / who was at fault?
MX: Japan and China were involved. Japan was absolutely in the wrong for murdering over 300,000 Chinese people and for outrageous crimes, such as rape. I remember there were pictures of the Japanese army and generals in our course book. We would draw them into ugly caricatures and make fun of them.
I: Do you think you learnt the whole story?
MX: We might have covered 80% of the whole story, but our books may have dodged some facts or events related to the massacre. For example, I doubt that the motivation of the Japanese for the rape of Nanjing was... their beastly nature. I found it interesting that the Japanese are always portrayed as perverts or beasts in our textbooks but, in fact, most (modern) Japanese people are nice and polite.

JASMINE HONG, 22

I: Did you learn about Nanjing at school?
JH: Yes, I did. It's a must-learn in modern Chinese history. Our teachers taught us: "Do not forget the shame so as to revive our nation." The Nanjing Massacre constitutes an important part of our national identity.
I: How was it referred to?
JH: Massacre in general, including rape, killing, arson and so on.
I: Who was involved / who was at fault?
JH: Japanese. Unlike some other historical incidents that may have different perspectives, the Nanjing Massacre was 100% caused by the Japanese.
I: Do you think you learnt the whole story?
JH: It's possible it wasn't the full extent. In my understanding, the powerful and rich have the privilege to lie. In this case, the Chinese didn't lie. I believe [the Chinese] about everything that happened during the Nanjing Massacre, including the rape and violence. What's planted deeply in my mind are two images from our textbooks. One was an old newspaper from back then that described a contest to kill 100 people using a sword. The horrifying descriptions continued to haunt me for years. Another image that shocked me was a Japanese soldier piercing a baby.

D.C. HU, 23

I: Did you learn about Nanjing at school?
DH: Yes, I remember learning it when I was younger, and also in high school. We focused especially on the number of people who died.
I: How was it referred to?
DH: The Nanjing Massacre.
I: Who was involved / who was at fault?
DH: Undoubtedly the Japanese were at fault in killing over 300,000 Chinese people brutally.
I: Do you think you learnt the whole story?
DH: Maybe there was something missed. But we know the end results of what happened. Our teacher always said that Japan might forget, but we won't. This is part of China's modern history.

JAPAN

YUKIKO SHINOZAKI, 22

I: Did you learn about Nanjing at school?

YS: Yes, we learned that Chinese citizens and soldiers disguised as ordinary people were massacred by the Japanese army, similar to what the Nazis did during the Holocaust.

I: What was the title?

YS: I forget. It was either the Nanjing Massacre or the Nanjing Incident.

I: Who was at fault?

YS: The old Japanese army.

I: Do you think you learnt the whole story?

YS: No, but I think it's important that people, including [me] and those who say they have little understanding of history, make an effort to continue learning so we can form our own opinions.

YOICHIRO MIKAMI, 20

I: Did you learn about Nanjing at school?

YM: We studied it in our world history class. I was taught that over 300,000 Chinese people were killed, but this was without any academic verification.

I: What was the title?

YM: The Nanjing Massacre by the Japanese army.

I: Who was at fault?

YM: In our class, the Japanese army and government were condemned.

I: Do you think you learnt the whole story?

YM: Not at all. I believe Japanese textbooks are self-destructive and overwhelmed by leftist ideology. Supposed facts about Nanjing are accepted by Japanese educational institutions because of Chinese propaganda.

TOMI NAKAMURA, 17

I: Did you learn about Nanjing at school?

TN: We did, but only for about 15 minutes. There were around five lines in the book and a picture of the Japanese army.

I: What was the title?

TN: A Massacre in Nanjing.

I: Who was at fault?

TN: I believe it was the Kwantung [Imperial Japanese] army.

I: Do you think you got to learn the whole story?

TN: I felt that only a small part of the story was written in our textbooks. Also, I think there's a difference between what's being taught in China and what we learn in Japan.

YUKA, 21

I: Did you learn about Nanjing at school?

Y: Yes, I remember studying it at junior high school. We were taught that the Japanese army captured Nanjing, killing many people. It was only one lesson.

I: What was the title?

Y: The Nanjing Incident, maybe.

I: Who was at fault?

Y: The teacher said the Japanese army had behaved badly. There was also something about the [Chinese] military leader Chiang Kai-shek, though I don't remember well.

I: Do you think you got to learn the whole story?

Y: We didn't study it deeply. I've read about people denying that it happened, but I don't know why.

Listening to these students, it's clear they were taught about Nanjing, but not in great detail. That doesn't necessarily mean teachers are trying to avoid the issue. The history curriculum in Japan covers many different eras and the focus is on memorising important dates rather than engaging in debate. A political dispute over which textbooks should include Nanjing, however, continues to rumble on in Japan.

Hannah Leung is based in Hong Kong. Matthew Hernon is based in Japan

The empire strikes back

47(01): 40/43 | DOI: 10.1177/0306422018770112

The Soviet Union may have fallen, but some of its attitudes on controlling history live on in Ukraine and Belarus, says **Andrei Aliaksandrau**

"**THE RED EMPIRE** is gone, but the Red Man, homo sovieticus, remains. He endures," Sviatlana Alieksievič said after winning the 2015 Nobel Prize in Literature. Born in Ukraine, she has lived most of her life in – and is a citizen of – Belarus.

Both countries share a complicated and painful history of being part of the Soviet Union. But they are both attempting to deal with understanding of, and control of, their past.

History books in Belarus have been completely republished four times since 1990, according to research by Aliaksiej Bratačkin, a historian from Minsk. Each change corresponded to a switch in political narrative to fit the objectives of those in charge.

At the beginning of the 1990s, the Soviet approaches to history were deemed "colonial and anti-Belarusian" and were changed to more nation-orientated ones. But it did not last long.

Alexander Lukašenko, the first – and so far the only – president of Belarus, came to power in 1994. All further changes in the official historical narrative have been defined by his political ambitions.

At first, Lukašenko tried to make friends with Russia, with a possible union of the two countries in mind. At that point, history books lost all national sentiment, refraining from deep analysis of previous conflicts.

But when Vladimir Putin came to power in Russia in 2000, and it became obvious the Belarus president was not going to succeed Yeltsin, the history books were rewritten to underline independence of Belarus and its differences from Russia.

"Now the authorities try to define the nation not through ethnicity but by belonging to the Belarusian state. A new model of such collective identity aims at fostering loyalty, not to the country or a nation but to the existing political regime," Bratačkin said.

World War II plays an extremely important role in the Belarusian state's historical narrative. It adopts the old Soviet name – the Great Patriotic War – and uses the notion of "the Great Victory" to depict the Belarusian state as an ancestor of one of the great powers that defeated fascism, thus transmitting the idea of that "greatness" to the present generation.

Lukašenko, who was born in 1954, is notorious for his emotional speech to war veterans, in which he told them his "father also died fighting in the World War II".

Ukraine, meanwhile, has had to deal with a war within its territory, beginning in 2014. After the Euromaidan revolution ousted President Viktor Yanukovych, Crimea was invaded and annexed by Russia, and some regions in the east have also been under the control of pro-Russian military groups, with strong evidence of Rus-

OPPOSITE: Guards stand near a monument in Minsk, Belarus, commemorating the Soviet victims of the war in Afghanistan, 2014

History textbooks "lost" most mentions of any anti-Russian figures and events in an effort not to annoy the Kremlin

sian regular troops supporting their military actions against Ukraine.

This country, too, has seen several attempts to change its official version of history. During Viktor Yanukovych's presidency (2010–2014), history textbooks "lost" most mentions of any anti-Russian figures and events in an effort not to annoy the Kremlin.

Stepan Bandera, one of the most prominent, and controversial, leaders of the Ukrainian independence movement, is a perfect example. He was sentenced to death by the Polish authorities in 1934; held in a Nazi concentration camp; and assassinated by the Soviet KGB in 1959. The Soviet – and now Russian – propaganda depicts Bandera as a "bandit" and a "fascist", while all his life he fought for the independence of his land.

"Ukraine is not divided now because of Bandera; it is divided because of the →

→ myth about Bandera that was invented by the Soviet propaganda," Volodymyr Via-trovych, the head of the Ukrainian Institute of National Memory, told Apostrophe TV.

"The policy of Russia is to reinstall its empire. And it does so by reinforcing the old Soviet myths and trying to reach people who like them. Thus, any attempts to challenge Soviet myths and Soviet interpretations of history anywhere see huge protests by Russia as they challenge its current policies."

In 2015, Ukraine adopted a series of laws that forbade propaganda of Soviet and Nazi totalitarian regimes, claiming they were equally culpable of crimes against humanity.

The country also updated its calendar of official holidays to reflect its political think-ing. Some of them are simply gone, such as the anniversary of the 1917 October Revolution (a state holiday in Russia and Belarus). Others got new meanings. Ukraine now celebrates 8 May as a day of memory and reconciliation, paying tribute to victims of World War II, rather than the sabre-rat-tling Victory Day that Russia and Belarus celebrate on 9 May.

"Russian propaganda often uses the term 'rewriting the history'. But this is not what is happening in Ukraine," said Svitlana Osip-chuk, a historian and lecturer at the Techni-cal University of Ukraine.

"We are going through the process of de-communisation of history, the change of the Soviet understanding of it. I can't say it is an easy process. But the most important thing I see is that history does not have the black-and-white narrative any more. There is now a good chance for an open public dialogue in Ukraine."

As Alieksievič said: "Sometimes I am not sure that I've finished writing the history of the "Red" man." ⊗

Andrei Aliaksandrau, a former Index on Censorship project officer, is publisher and editor of online magazine Belarusian Journal (journalby.com)

|||||||||||||||||||||||||||||||||||||||||||||||||||||||||

THE WHOLE TRUTH

Ukraine needs to accept all its past, however ugly, writes STEPHEN KOMARNYCKYJ

Ukraine suffered greatly at the hands of the Nazis and the Soviets, leaving 13.5 million of its citizens dead. It owes a duty to the victims to tell their story. And yet that's not what's happening.

The latest example of how the Ukrainian government is covering up aspects of its past concerns British historian Sir Anthony Beevor. In January, the Russian translation of his bestselling book, Stalingrad, which won the 1999 Samuel Johnson prize and ex-plores the history of the World War II battle, was banned in Ukraine. This followed the passing of a law in 2016 that banned the im-port of books from Russia if they contained "anti-Ukrainian" content.

Beevor's book was prohibited on the grounds that it might incite "inter-ethnic, ra-cial and religious hostility".

CREDIT: Alexander Zemlianichenko/Rex

Serhiy Oliyinyk, head of the Ukrainian Committee for State TV and Radio Broadcasting's licensing and distribution control department, told Radio Free Europe that the ban was imposed because of a passage about how 90 Jewish children were shot by Ukrainian militia. "It's a provocation," he said.

Although the ban was ultimately overturned, it left the impression Ukraine was suppressing debate about its past.

There are some signs that the government is seeking to do just that. This was a directive enshrining the study of the Organisation of Ukrainian Nationalists' contribution to the independence struggle within the education system. This promotes a history that masks the OUN's collaboration with the Nazis.

Ukraine has been tackling awareness of its Soviet crimes, but some recent laws hamper discussion about collaboration with the Nazis and its involvement in the Holocaust. They also prohibit questioning the legitimacy of the independence struggle.

The Organisation of Ukrainian Nationalists is seemingly protected from criticism. There is evidence, however, that the OUN participated in the Holocaust.

Uilleam Blacker, a lecturer in comparative culture of Russia and eastern Europe at University College London, noted that 2016 commemorations for the Babi Yar massacre, in which tens of thousands of Jews were slaughtered in 1941, "avoided the problem of local collaborators and nationalist organisations".

Olesya Khromeychuk, a fellow in history at the University of East Anglia, said these measures are demolishing the existing eclectic memory of World War II and replacing it with a "simplistic account". She stresses that the laws legitimise individuals such as Roman Shukhevych, the leader of the UPA, the OUN's military wing, which worked with the Nazis.

If Ukraine doesn't allow space for a more honest reading of its recent tragic history, we'll see more bans in the future.

Stephen Komarnyckyj is an editor and translator of Ukrainian literature

Staging dissent

47(01): 44/46 | DOI: 10.1177/0306422018770113

Fifty years ago, the UK government abolished the role of the Lord Chamberlain in censoring plays, but vigilance is still needed, writes actor and director **Simon Callow**

THE FIGHT TO abolish censorship in the theatre was a long and at times bitter one, descending at the end into absurdity, which was entirely fitting, since that is how it had started, in 1737, with Prime Minister Sir Robert Walpole sensationally flourishing a copy of a play called The Golden Rump in parliament. The piece was derived, cried Walpole, from a scurrilous cartoon in which the owner of the eponymous posterior was clearly King George II, his pot-bellied Chief Magician unquestionably Walpole, and the woman inserting "a Golden Tube… with a large Bladder at the End" into her husband's gilded bottom was very obviously Queen Caroline.

No such play had been announced for presentation, and no author was acknowledged as having written it, so it was widely assumed that Walpole's cronies had cooked it up; nevertheless, quoting ever more salaciously from the *soi-disant* play, Walpole roused his fellow MPs to heights of horror and indignation and a draconian bill, the Licensing Act, was passed in the Commons.

From the outset Walpole's various administrations had been accused of corruption and venality, for which they were duly lambasted in print and on stage by the satirists of the day, among them the fledgling dramatist Henry Fielding, who from 1734 had turned his ferocious talents with increasing savagery onto Walpole personally. Walpole finally snapped, rushing the bill into parliament. It required

that henceforth all plays must be submitted to an Examiner of the Stage, an officer of the Lord Chamberlain who would be given powers to forbid "as often as he shall see fit" any dramatic piece "for hire, gain, or reward".

In the House of Lords, it ran up against the formidable Lord Chesterfield. "A Power lodged in the hands of one single Man, to judge and determine, without any Limitation, without any Control or Appeal," said Chesterfield, "is a sort of power unknown to our Laws, inconsistent with our Constitution. It is a higher, a more absolute power than we trust even to the King himself; therefore I think we ought not to vest any such Power in His Majesty's Chamberlain." More was at stake, he insisted, than the well-being of writers and actors: "The Stage, my lords, and the Press, are two of our out-sentries; if we remove them – if we hood-wink them – if we throw them in Fetters – the enemy may surprise us." He was certain, he said, that his fellow Lords would reject such a bill; but he was wrong, and we lived with the consequences for nearly 250 years.

Fielding immediately stopped writing for the stage and turned to the novel; incessantly harried by the censor, those writers who stuck by the theatre relapsed into a sentimental and tepid vein which could cause no offence. The censor's work was done for him: the cop was no longer in the street; he was in the writers' heads. By the end of the century,

CREDIT: Elina Kansikas/Index on Censorship

the authorities' hysterical anxiety about the contagiousness of the French revolution made them unusually pro-active: any play which alluded to oppression or patriotism was cut or suppressed; the anodyne Charles the First by Mary Russell Mitford, and Alasco by Martin Archer Shee were banned outright; many others were brutally censored without explanation. Europe was at first the source of all anxiety: then Scandinavia and Russia. The "advanced theatre" of Ibsen and Strindberg, dealing frankly with social issues, was a particular menace. Banning left, right and centre, the censor suppressed Ibsen's Ghosts, Tolstoy's The Power of Darkness, Brieux's Damaged Goods – which dealt directly with syphilis – plus home-grown plays like Shaw's Mrs Warren's Profession and Edward Garnett's The Breaking Point, about a single mother. This authoritarian philistinism caused the poet Swinburne to remark that the Lord Chamberlain had exposed the English stage "to the contempt of civilised Europe".

As the 19th century advanced, dramatists started fighting back, becoming cockier and more cunning. W S Gilbert cheekily put the Lord Chamberlain on stage as The Lord High Disinfectant. Then writers stumbled on the notion of members'-only theatres, which made the first performances of Ghosts possible, as well as of Shaw's Widowers' Houses, which dealt head-on with property racketeering. As late as the 1930s, creating a club was the only way in which the very mild biographical play Oscar Wilde, which starred the eminently respectable Robert Morley, could be performed. Homosexuality – "the forbidden subject" as the Chamberlain's office coyly referred to it – was one of the many key facts of life which they attempted to keep from the British public, but once the Wolfenden Report appeared in 1957, in a blaze of publicity, the game was up.

From then on, the censors were fighting a losing battle. Entrenched in St James's Palace, they grew further and further out of touch with modern life and developments

in the theatre, spending their days trying to bowdlerise the plays they received, proposing baffling alternatives to phrases that offended them: "For 'wind from a duck's behind,'" said one report, "substitute 'wind from Mount Zion'." "The Detergent song. Omit: 'You get all the dirt off the tail of your shirt.' Substitute 'You get all the dirt off the front of your shirt'." Managers increasingly resorted to converting their premises into club theatres; London's Royal Court, leading the attack on behalf of new writing, became stubbornly defiant. John Osborne eventually exploded. "I cannot agree," he furiously wrote to them concerning his 1960 play Luther, "to any of the cuts demanded, under any circumstances. Nor will I agree to any possible substitutions. I don't write plays to have them rewritten by someone else." He won; only a couple of cuts were demanded. The Lord Chamberlain was palpably weakening; finally, the Royal Court's

ABOVE: Actor Simon Callow at Index's Stand Up for Satire show, 2017

If we throw them in Fetters – the enemy may surprise us

pably weakening; finally, the Royal Court's determination not to be deflected at any cost from presenting the plays of Edward Bond, with their viscerally disturbing imagery, confounded them. Threats of prosecution only further demonstrated their weakness; in due course an all-party parliamentary committee unanimously concluded that the censor must go. Only the Society of West End Theatre Managers, who liked the legal protection the Chamberlain's office provided, pleaded →

ABOVE: Cartoon of the Golden Rump, the infamous, possibly fake, play that Sir Robert Walpole used to pass the Licensing Act of 1737, creating theatre censorship

→ for its retention. Lord Cobbold, the incumbent Chamberlain, frantically lobbied for special clauses to protect the royal family, the Archbishop of Canterbury and the Pope, but to no avail: he was abruptly consigned to theatrical oblivion.

The abolition of the office of censor has not, of course, eliminated all censorship. The theatre, as Osborne famously remarked, is a minority art with a majority influence, and someone is always trying to hi-jack it. Private prosecutions are possible, though the failure of the most notorious, Mary Whitehouse's determination to suspend the run of Howard Brenton's The Romans in Britain, has had a discouraging effect on subsequent attempts. But from both left and right of the political spectrum, and from religious groups, there have been protests, some violent, against theatre companies held to be offensive in some way. Protest, of course, is an entirely legitimate democratic activity, though it has

from time to time overshot its mark, most famously in Birmingham when the play Behzti, set partly in a Sikh temple, was shut down by the violence of the protests, driving writer Gupreet Kaur Bahtti into hiding.

Similarly, any Israeli theatre company, no matter what its position, comes to the United Kingdom at its peril. The Israeli National Theatre, the Habima, was disrupted when it brought its production of The Merchant of Venice to Shakespeare's Globe in 2012; two years later in Edinburgh The City, performed by the group Incubator, whose remit is to promote Israeli-Palestinian interaction, was closed down because police claimed that they could not guarantee the company's safety. They returned last year, again to vociferous protests, but the show went on attended by a tiny number of harassed theatregoers.

And the most ominous form of censorship – self-censorship – is always with us; in an age of trolling tweeters and acid in the face, it can be frightening to defy the common wisdom. Courage is required if the theatre wants to continue to be one of the out-sentries, as Chesterfield put it. And it requires sharp and even-handed vigilance from everyone else. ⊗

Simon Callow is an actor, director and writer. He played the Master of the Revels, the Elizabethan theatre censor, in the film Shakespeare In Love

PLAY BY THE RULES

• Plays were not permitted licences under the Lord Chamberlain's censorship rules for odd reasons. A licence was once refused because the leading lady entered a tent "nude under her clothes".
• If a licence were granted, it was after numerous cuts and revisions, such as The Bedsitting Room by Spike Milligan and John Antrobus, in 1963, which included the

change: "the mock priest must not wear a crucifix on his snorkel".
• Thanks to the Lord Chamberlain's rules on what could be depicted in a play, topics such as religion were heavily censored. No plays about Queen Victoria were permitted before the late 1930s.
• The phrase "up periscope" was banned as the Lord Chamberlain felt it was too suggestive and could lead people to "commit buggery". *Danyaal Yasin*

Eye of the storm

47(01): 47/49 | DOI: 10.1177/0306422018770114

Omar Mohammed, aka **Mosul Eye**, was one of the main sources for the outside world to see what life was like inside Mosul, Iraq. Here he explains how he risked his life – and watched others being killed – in the name of historical research

THE ROOM WHERE I wrote Mosul Eye was one thin wall away from the house where a senior Isis fighter lived. There I sat documenting the group's brutality to the world, close enough to the militants that it was possible to hear them speak. As a scholar, it was my mission to deconstruct their historical narrative, despite the great danger of doing so. Writing history under such a totalitarian ideology was an act of resistance to the group's destruction of Mosul's multicultural identity and heritage. Now that Isis have finally left Mosul and the city is rebuilding, I hope my work will be invaluable.

The turning point for me – and for Mosul – was 13 June 2014, just days after Isis occupied the city, when a document of 16 articles entitled the Constitution of Medina [or Madina Document] was issued to rule the city. This made it evident that the extremists were weaponising history to legitimise their actions. I knew we faced a crisis of knowledge among the public, where history would be abused to encourage the hatred of other groups.

Isis carried out a systematic destruction of Mosul's identity. First, they forced the city's non-Muslim inhabitants to flee, destroying their heritage in an effort to remove them from the city's history. Then came the destruction of ancient Assyrian and cultural sites. After this brutality against Mosul's non-Islamic history, they shifted to the Muslim community, where they began to systematically destroy Islamic archaeological sites, as well as museums, libraries and manuscripts.

They also took aim at Mosul's linguistic heritage. Where the city once had a rich, peaceful vocabulary of everyday words and phrases, the group implemented a vocabulary of violence and social division. They brought their own medieval dictionary. We began to hear *diwan* instead of *waizara* (ministry), *hisba* instead of *shurta* (police), *bayt al-mal* (house of money) instead of *al-bank al-markazi* (central bank). New labels were applied to the social classes: *ansar* were the Isis "local" members and fighters; *muhajirun* the Isis foreign fighters; *munasirun* were those who supported and welcomed Isis but were not members. Opponents who were jihadists but were against Isis were *mukhalifun*. Finally, *āmma* were the lower classes and were against Isis. My family and I were *āmma*.

In the early days of the occupation, I wrote posts on Mosul Eye's social media accounts. At that time, the internet was disconnected by the Iraqi government and the only way to get connected was through Isis-controlled channels. You had to apply for internet access through them, giving away personal details about yourself in the process – something I could not do. Fortunately, a friend filled out a fake application on my behalf.   →

My journals became a timebomb that might explode at any moment, leading to the death of me and my entire family

→ I then wrote anonymously (it has been only in the last few months that I have revealed my real identity, living away from Mosul in relative safety) and I wrote often.

In tasking myself with recording this history, I had to confront not only my own fear of death – for anyone who deviated from documenting the official version of events could be killed – but also the version of history Isis appropriated about my city. In times

when oppressors hold all the power and are carrying out extraordinary acts of violence, what can a single person do?

I documented everything I saw firsthand, wandering through the city's streets and markets and speaking to people for hours. Having lost my job teaching history at Mosul university, I worked small part-time jobs – as a baker, at a grocery store and sometimes as a taxi driver.

Through these roles I witnessed many events and would return home to transcribe them as a historian. I forced myself to go to live executions so that I could hear the names called out of those who were being killed and what reason was given. I went to hospitals where doctors told me about the

have three records of what was happening to my city. Death was so near. If I were to be killed, it had to be for something. Protecting these records therefore became key. Because I was writing about daily events, I needed regular access to my journals. The threat that Isis could search my home at any moment and find these records was all too real. They routinely searched homes for any reason. My

Documenting history in such a context is a battle for knowledge

journals became a time bomb that might explode at any moment, leading to the death of me and my entire family.

So I devised a way to protect them, hiding them well in my home. But I was plagued by the fear that no one would know where they were if I were killed, and sharing a copy with anyone would expose my work as an undercover historian. Since 2013, I had been corresponding with a friend who was also a scholar. I decided to share my journals with him electronically without telling him I was Mosul Eye. He emailed me to say they were printed and safe. He probably understood the reason I was sending them.

My battle since June 2014 has been to reverse what Isis has tried to implant in the consciousness of Mosul's residents with the only weapon I have as a historian – writing history. The social, cultural and historical destruction wrought by the group will impact the city for centuries to come. Documenting history in such a context is a battle for knowledge: to develop the critical thinking capacity of the individual as a resistance to tyranny and to protect knowledge for the future. Now that Isis have left, I hope a more comprehensive history of the city can follow. ⊗

Omar Mohammed runs the website Mosul Eye and is currently doing his PhD in the history of Mosul in the 19th and 20th centuries

rape (and sometimes subsequent death from injuries) of Yazidi girls.

To know how decisions were being made, however, I needed access to Isis members. How can one get information from them without being accused of spying and then summarily executed? I chose to play a high-stakes game. Having read, studied and taught Islamic history, I used my knowledge of Islam to debate them, opening a channel of communication. I went to Mosul's mosques dressed like them and listened to Isis members, waiting for the opportunity to engage in discussions with them and control the debate. I recorded all the information I had gathered, scanned the handwritten documents and also typed up my notes so as to

MAIN: The ancient city of Nimrud, which contained the tombs of Assyrian kings, lies in ruins, November 2016. Just one of many historical sites destroyed under Isis rule

CREDIT: Michael Grant Travel/Alamy

Desert defenders

47(01): 50/52 I DOI: 10.1177/0306422018770116

Argentina's government still tries to gloss over the battle which wiped out the majority of its indigenous population, says **Lucia He**

EARLIER THIS YEAR, Argentina's President Mauricio Macri said at the World Economic Forum that "in South America, all of us are descendants of Europeans".

The statement was false – more than 22 million indigenous people live in Latin America – but to many in the region, Macri's statement didn't come as a surprise.

In Latin America, Argentina is often (negatively) perceived by its neighbours as the region's European country.

Unlike most of its neighbours, which all have significant indigenous or black populations, Argentina's population is 97% white, or *mestizo*, mixed European and Amerindian descent. This homogeneity can be traced back to a single event in the 1870s that changed the course of the country's history: the Conquest of the Desert.

For more than a decade, this campaign led by General Julio Argentino Roca sought to establish Argentine dominance in Patagonia, a territory inhabited by diverse groups of indigenous communities. Thousands of indigenous people were killed, and tens of thousands more were displaced, allowing

Argentina to expand its territory to its current frontier with Chile.

Up to this day, the Argentine government still takes care to position the event as a legitimate war that sought to establish the country's sovereignty.

A sign of how the government sees the importance of the event is illustrated by a comment by Education Minister Esteban Bullrich, in 2016, who emphasised the importance of investing in education by saying: "We can't have independence without education. This is the new Conquest of the Desert, but with education instead of swords."

Yet a growing number of academics and journalists see the conquest as a genocide.

According to Carlos Martínez Sarasola, an Argentine anthropologist, up to half of the indigenous people living in Patagonia were murdered during the conquest. Marcelo Valko details in his book Pedagogia de la Desmemoria (The Pedagogy of Forgetting) the process during the conquest through which a group of 3,000 indigenous people were put into concentration camps and forcefully baptised and tortured.

"We've been told a story that is very different from the real events that took place. It was those who benefited from the conquest who wrote this story. If you were one of the 1,845 families that received a total of 42 million hectares from Julio Roca, he's going to be your benefactor forever. These are the same families that dominate today's politics," said Valko in a recent interview with the newspaper Conclusión.

Throughout the country's history, the Argentine state has been able to keep a one-sided narrative on the events of the Conquest of the Desert and its impact, by idealising it and its leaders and suppressing and marginalising the voices of the remaining indigenous communities.

The portrayals of Roca as a hero are abundant in everyday life. In 1992, the government introduced a new design for the country's 100 peso note commemorating him. The bills display Roca's portrait on one side and a full picture of the army leading the military campaign on the other. A design featuring Eva Peron was introduced in 2012, but millions of the Roca notes are still in circulation.

Roca's presence is not only inside Argentine wallets but also on the streets. There are at least 36 statues commemorating the general across the country, along with dozens of streets, avenues and public schools.

Besides commemorating Roca, another way in which the Argentine government has been able to legitimise the Conquest of the Desert has been to perpetuate the idea of indigenous communities as "others" through education and the media.

"The conquest established an official narrative: the idea that indigenous people were dangerous savages, that the conquest was

Up to half of the indigenous people living in Patagonia were murdered during the conquest

a fight between civilisation and barbarism. And unfortunately, this ideology still persists until this day," said Sarasola.

According to a study that analysed high school curriculums in Argentina from 1956 to 1980, the Conquest of the Desert was largely taught as an event that legitimised the Argentine state and allowed the country to become an agricultural superpower in the decades following the conquest. Indigenous communities were portrayed as an obstacle for the territorial consolidation of the state and the promotion of "civilisation". Words used in textbooks and history classes to characterise them included "savages", "barbaric", "primitives", "lazy" and "aggressive".

In a study published last year, anthropologist Mariano Nagy concluded that these notions imposed in the traditional school system in Argentina continue with no →

→ major change or questioning: "Nowadays, schools display these same old premises of savagery, barbarism, the backwardness of indigenous communities and the inexorable progress achieved after the extinction of indigenous peoples."

According to Nagy, this notion has stuck in the collective mind, and students agree with this analysis. "My personal experience on the issue of the Conquest of the Desert is dismally limited," said Azul Cibils, a 17-year-old high school student in Buenos Aires. "We learnt about it in the first year of secondary school and, even though we talked about how many people were murdered and about how Roca was an oligarch, the discussion didn't go much deeper. We simply talked

A group of 3,000 indigenous people were put into concentration camps and forcefully baptised and tortured

about what the conquest meant for the Argentine republic in terms of land gain. I frankly believe the issue should be taught in much more detail and depth."

Another study conducted in 2010 about the portrayal of indigenous communities by the media showed that, when covering territorial conflicts between indigenous Mapuche communities and the Argentine government, it often questioned the origins of Mapuches and portrayed them as land-grabbers and violent extremists. Last year, in the face of escalating conflict between security forces and Mapuche communities, the Mapuche were accused of being originally from Chile, and some characterised them as terrorists.

"Unfortunately, racism and discrimination towards indigenous communities or any other type of minorities are a part of Argentine society. This is probably a consequence

of the way history has been taught to us," said Sarasola.

"Argentina's indigenous communities were completely left out during the democratic transition in the country," said Diego Morales, director at the Center for Legal and Social Studies, a non-profit organisation working on indigenous issues.

In 2006, Argentina's Congress passed a law that required the state to conduct an official survey on the lands inhabited by indigenous communities. The law introduced the survey as a first step towards the formalisation of their land rights. However, a study published this year showed that, 11 years after the sanctioning of the law, only half of the communities had been surveyed.

"Argentina hasn't been able to establish a serious state policy that recognises indigenous communities and that goes beyond changes in government. When you don't implement a concrete state policy, you have a policy of denial," said Sarasola.

This has resulted in escalating conflicts between the Argentine state and indigenous communities. According to a survey conducted by Amnesty International's local chapter, there are currently as many as 264 ongoing conflicts involving indigenous communities. Last year, a conflict between Argentine authorities and a group of Mapuches escalated into violence and culminated with the death of 28-year-old indigenous rights activist Santiago Maldonado.

Human rights activists and indigenous groups believe that in order for Argentina's indigenous communities to be able to fully claim back their rights, the country's historical narrative needs to be amended.

In the words of Osvaldo Bayer, a writer and journalist: "Our heroes have to be those who, in our history, fought for the right to life of all, and not the ones who, for ambition of power and property, stripped the life of the children of our land." ⊗

Lucia He is a journalist based in Buenos Aires

Buried treasures

47(01): 53/54 I DOI: 10.1177/0306422018770117

Historians tracking down Britain's historical documents are encountering a crisis, says **David Anderson**, who exposed a government cover-up of torture during Kenya's Mau Mau Uprising

THE BRITISH GOVERNMENT talks of its commitment to "open government" and the transparency and accountability this implies. Yet in recent years, several scandals have emerged surrounding the retention of historical documents, or their destruction, by government departments. Historians in Britain should be concerned, and action is needed to better protect the records from which future histories can be written.

The introduction of a 20-year-rule making formerly secret documents public, and revelations of massive holdings of documents held by departments in infringement of the UK's Public Records Act, have created a crisis of formidable proportions. The system is struggling to cope, and government departments can't deal with the backlog. This is made worse by limited resources for record management, especially in the last five years, due to budget cuts. Austerity means that even those who would like to pass records on to archives don't have the capacity.

In May 2013, the first legal case bringing to light the scale of government secrecy took place. The British government made an out-of-court settlement with 5,228 Kenyans who had been tortured whilst in British detention during the Mau Mau Uprising of the 1950s.

This was an armed rebellion among the Kikuyu in central Kenya, aimed at bringing colonial white rule to an end. The rebels killed 32 white settlers, and murdered over 3,000 Africans accused of collaboration. The British counter-insurgency crushed the uprising, resulting in an estimated 25,000 deaths and the detention of 80,000 Kikuyu suspected of rebel sympathies.

The payments in 2013 marked the culmination of a legal campaign that had spanned more than a decade. Access to crucial documentary evidence was a bone of contention throughout this protracted case, with London lawyers Leigh Day making repeated requests for the government to release records.

Historians, too, had endeavoured to track down these documents. These requests met with deflection, denial and, ultimately, deceit, as the British government sought to keep critical evidence out of the hands of those who might use it for legal redress.

The breakthrough in the Mau Mau case came in December 2010, when the High Court ordered the Foreign and Commonwealth Office to locate and release the documents described in a witness statement I had submitted through Leigh Day. The FCO now miraculously "found" the documents which they denied had existed and late in January 2011, Leigh Day's legal team received the first of a huge tranche of historical papers. It was admitted that these 1,500 files had been illegally and secretly removed from Kenya before the country's independence in 1963. The documents provided critical evidence supporting claims of torture and abuse. →

ABOVE: A police-man guards Mau Mau tribesmen, Nairobi, Kenya, 1954

→ And there were more revelations to come. In April 2011, a statement announced that a further cache of documents relating to 36 former British colonies and dependencies would be released – more than 24,000 files.

Then, in 2013, a further 1.2 million "retained materials" emerged. These included papers dealing with Nazis at the end of World War II, as well as Cold War spying.

There is a further sinister aspect: the FCO did not consider these materials "searchable" under the Freedom of Information Act. If a document is not listed, it cannot be found. In effect, the documents did not officially exist. This raises the question of whether other government departments may also hold collections of documents that are not listed.

The preservation of Britain's historical records is primarily protected through an act of parliament passed 60 years ago. The Public Records Act (1958) sets down the legal procedures that government departments must follow in retaining, destroying or releasing documents in the public domain. Written long before digitisation, and decades before anyone thought of freedom of information as a right, the 1958 act is archaic. Despite this, government departments are required to work with The National Archives, at Kew, within the terms of the act.

This creaking act has been augmented in important ways by two more recent pieces of legislation. The first, dating from 2000, is the Freedom of Information Act, which allows individuals to request the release of any government document. The second is the Constitutional Reform and Governance Act of 2010. This reduced the long-standing 30-year-rule on document release to 20 years, massively increasing the workload of those who make documents public.

A stream of press stories from 2014 suggesting there might be other hidden document caches were summed up in the publication of Ian Cobain's book The History Thieves (2016). Cobain saw secrecy as a "fiercely protected norm" of British government. This view was evident in the reaction of the Cameron government to the accidental release, in January 2014, of documents relating to British assistance for an operation by the Indian army at the Golden Temple in Amritsar in 1984. These showed that the Thatcher government had been complicit in a military action that resulted in a massacre in which hundreds died. Cameron's reaction to the leak was to ask why the management of British documents had been so careless as to release this information.

The Golden Temple scandal led directly to the setting up of a far-reaching Cabinet Office enquiry, which makes for alarming reading. It identified at least six other departments as holding large "legacy collections". The Ministry of Defence had the most significant backlog. In all these cases, the departments lacked lists of the files concerned.

The inability, or unwillingness, of departments to comply with their legal requirements under the Public Records Act gives a hollow ring to British claims of "open government". Historians are right to be suspicious that the past is liable to censorship by the actions, or inactions, of government. ⊗

David Anderson is an author and a professor of history at the University of Warwick

CREDIT: Popperfoto/Getty

Masters of none

47(01): 55/56 I DOI: 10.1177/0306422018770118

There are two ways of understanding the concept of mastering history. In not attempting to understand why things happened you fail to learn from them, writes leading academic **Bernt Hagtvet**

THE GERMANS ARE good at multi-layered concepts. *Vergangenheitsbewältigung* is a case in point. It literally means "mastery of the past". But underneath there is an interesting ambiguity. *"Bewältigung"* can mean mastery of the past in the sense that you control history, impose your interpretation of the past, to the exclusion of other voices. Subjugate it.

Vladimir Putin's view of the Soviet past may be classified as an example of this sense of mastery. Under Putin, new monuments of Stalin are being erected across the country. It's just one measure that seeks to highlight the military and technological advances that happened under the Soviet leader's rule, and which whitewash his repression and terror. It feeds the narrative of a great Russian past. You master history to your own advantage

and exploit it selectively for contemporary political purposes.

The other interpretation of the concept of mastery is to "confront yourself with history", to look history honestly in the face, warts and all.

Concretely, this involves a moral reckoning. Coming to terms with history. In Germany's case this has meant an open discussion about National Socialism (Nazism), fully recognising its criminal nature and its popular support, with no attempt to historicise this period of German history. It also means seeing history as a warning for the future.

In contemporary Poland, as well as in Hungary, this *Vergangenheitsbewältigung*, in both senses of the word, has been going on for a while. Since gaining power in 2015 the Law and Justice (PiS) in Poland has stacked the →

→ courts with its own people, sought to control the media, purged and politicised the civil service and intimidated intellectuals.

True to form, in regimes of this kind the populist and nationalist government in Warsaw is trying to forge a uniform interpretation of Polish history. In a recent law Warsaw has made it illegal to write the words, "Polish concentration camps" (see p35).

Polish citizens excavated valuables from the graves of Jews killed in the camps and exhibited their bones as badges of victory

This is quite unnecessary. Every thinking person knows that the concentration camps were a Nazi invention set up on Polish-occupied territory. Any discussion of this kind must be fought with words and facts, not threats of imprisonment.

More importantly, the same laws make it illegal to allege that Poles assisted the Nazis. The laws make exceptions for Holocaust witnesses and academics, but it is clear that this provision may easily create an atmosphere of intimidation among journalists and scholars who want an honest confrontation with Poland's past, including Polish collaboration with Nazis.

A case in point is recorded by the Polish sociologist Jan Gross in his book Neighbours (2001). In 1941 local people in the village of Jedwabne locked hundreds of Jews in a barn and set it on fire. People who tried to flee through the windows were shot. Gross has been hounded by the Polish authorities and threatened with all kinds of sanctions and smear campaigns for his honesty.

In a later work, Fear, Gross recorded instances of anti-Semitism and pogroms after the war. In Golden Harvest (2012), he documented how Polish citizens excavated valuables from the graves of Jews killed in the camps and exhibited their bones as badges of victory, much like football teams display their soccer balls in photos.

The interpretation the government seems to be spreading is an amalgam of hero worship and attacks on victimhood, casting sceptics in the role of traitor. The government wants to portray itself as the only guarantor of the honour of the Polish nation. Instead its lawmaking has led to deep rifts with the EU and the laughter and disbelief of other nations.

This is such an unnecessary struggle. Poland was one of the worst victims of Nazi barbarism, with about six million dead (including more than three million Polish Jews). Polish history is full of stories about Poles helping Jews under the most awful conditions. The country has countless tales of extreme heroism in assisting Jews, such as Jan Karski who went into the Warsaw ghetto to see with his own eyes how the Nazis killed the Jews. He found his way to London and Washington to alert the Allies of the horrors.

Trying to cleanse history like this is simply dumb. When governments try to cement one interpretation of historical truths to serve political purposes, it tends to be counterproductive.

The Polish government does not understand that acting like a policeman of interpretations will have unexpected effects and produce resistance, which will undercut its intentions and hopes. This is rather elementary. The PiS has performed political and intellectual striptease.

Now the government is ostracised abroad. Its attempt to cleanse history in the first sense of *Vergangenheitsbewältigung* has backfired.

At home support has surged. But in failing to master history fully it is depriving its citizens of a proper understanding and ability to learn from Poland's past. ⊗

Bernt Hagtvet teaches political science in Oslo, Norway, and is a leading expert on European fascism. He is chairman of the board for the Oslo-based Human Rights House Foundation

SPECIAL
REPORT

Naming history's forgotten fighters

47(01): 57/59 I DOI: 10.1177/0306422018770119

Many of those at the forefront of the anti-apartheid campaign are being erased from South Africa's history, argues **Raymond Joseph**

SIXTY YEARS AFTER a split opened up between the African National Congress and what was to become the Pan Africanist Congress, the PAC has largely been written out of South African history with the ruling party taking the credit for liberating South Africa from the shackles of apartheid. In fact, it was the PAC that led the historic anti-pass law campaign – protests against an internal "passport" system that controlled and limited movement – which culminated in the Sharpeville Massacre, on 21 March 1960. The incident left 69 people dead and at least 180 seriously wounded after police opened fire on peaceful anti-pass demonstrators outside the Sharpeville police station.

Despite its key role in the war against apartheid, in 2018 knowledge of the PAC's part in the struggle is fading, its leaders are hardly remembered and some of its fighters remain in prison decades after the end of apartheid.

The party adopted a hardline stance in its submission to the Truth and Reconciliation Commission and very few combatants in its armed wing, the Azanian People's Liberation Army, were granted amnesty for crimes which, they argued, were politically motivated. As recently as 2015, the PAC claimed that more than 100 of its members were still

in prison. Some have been freed over the years, but it is not clear how many still remain behind bars.

Noor Nieftagodien, a professor of history at the University of the Witwatersrand who heads up its history workshop, said: "Between 1960 and 1963, the PAC, in the minds of some, was seen as an alternative to the ANC. Yet they were still unable to challenge the ANC's dominance.

"Once the ANC came to power, it instituted projects that justified why it was in power. They made it seem that it was inevitable that they would (come to power)."

Explaining how new governments represent – and often misrepresent – history, Nieftagodien said: "Those who are in power want to demonstrate this in various ways. Symbolically, they want to show they are in charge. In South Africa, a lot of names, even some of a politically-neutral nature, had to go ... it was inevitable. In the initial period of a new government, the party in power will try and impose its own history. But I think, by and large, we are past the renaming process."

At one point in the late 1950s the PAC threatened to overshadow the ANC and become the dominant black-led party in South Africa. But by the time of the 1994 general election that brought the ANC to power, →

57
INDEXONCENSORSHIP.ORG

→ the once-mighty PAC was a spent force. It garnered just 1.25% of the vote and five seats in parliament thanks to South Africa's proportional representation system.

In comparison, the ANC won 262 seats and a huge 62.6% of the votes cast. Today the PAC has only one seat in parliament after receiving just 0.017% of the vote in the 2014 general election.

In the wake of Sharpeville, the government launched a draconian crackdown, ban-

As recently as 2015, the PAC claimed that more than 100 of its members were still in prison

ning the ANC and PAC using the Unlawful Organisations Act. Leaders were arrested and many people fled into exile to avoid being incarcerated.

Just how much the PAC has been forgotten was illustrated by last year's renaming of De Waal Drive, a key highway into Cape Town, after the PAC's Philip Kgosana. As a 17-year-old, Kgosana helped avert almost certain bloodshed after a 30,000 strong march to parliament against the pass laws in March 1960 threatened to end in death.

Some complained about the name change, and it was clear that many people had never heard of Kgosana, who died a year before the renaming. Former Cape Times editor Tony Heard, who covered the march as a young reporter and who championed the renaming campaign, said: "It was important for me that we remember a brave man who played an important role in our history. History is all we've got, because we do not know the future. It is not only shaped by organisations and ideologies, it is also shaped by people."

As the National Party changed names to celebrate their heroes when they swept to power in 1948, the ANC has done the same.

Name changes have been controversial and highly-contested terrain in a post-apartheid South Africa, with some people accusing the ANC of largely renaming roads and buildings in towns and cities it controlled after its own cadres.

There was outrage in Amanzimtoti, near Durban, when the ANC-led council renamed a road in the seaside hamlet after Andrew Zondo, an Umkhonto we Sizwe activist who was convicted of planting a limpet mine at a shopping centre on the same stretch of road two days before Christmas in 1985. The explosion killed five people, including children aged two, eight and 16, and left more than 40 people injured. Zondo was subsequently convicted of murder and hanged in 1986.

Instead of reflecting Durban's long history, most of the renamed roads commemorated local ANC members, many of them unknown outside party circles. It also created confusion and, until a few years ago, both the old and the new names appeared alongside one another on road signs. Many older people still refer to these roads by their old names.

At times, the renaming process became heated and at one stage the opposition Democratic Party hauled the ANC-led eThekwini Municipality to court and successfully forced it to reverse the renaming of several roads in Durban.

The renaming process also seemed to involve no proper research outside of the ANC's own history. For example, Edwin Swales Drive, on Durban's Bluff, was named after a South African bomber pilot who was awarded the Victoria Cross for bravery during World War II. The road was renamed after ANC combatant Solomon Mhlangu, who was convicted of murder and hanged in 1979.

Interestingly, name changes in Cape Town, which is governed by the opposition Democratic Alliance, reflect a wide range of people from across the political spectrum. There you will find Nelson Mandela Boulevard; Helen Suzman Boulevard, named after a woman who at one stage was the sole MP representing the liberal Progressive Party in

Parliament; FW de Klerk Boulevard, after South Africa's last white president who freed Mandela and unbanned the ANC; and Robert Sobukwe Drive, after the quietly-spoken teacher who led a breakaway from the ANC to form the PAC.

Ben Turok, a former ANC MP, was one of the 90 people charged with treason alongside Mandela and other leaders of the Congress Movement. Asked if history had been unkind to the PAC, he said: "History makes a judgment; it reflects what you did and what you didn't do. MK [Umkhonto we Sizwe] developed an army of 30,000. The PAC, in later years, just talked.

"But the PAC and Poqo [its former armed wing] deserve credit for awakening the feelings of struggle in the 1950s."

Omar Badsha, a historian who heads up the South African History Online project, said: "History is a very powerful way of controlling and changing people's perceptions of what happened and to justify it. It is also possible to create great silences.

"The PAC deserves credit just like any other organisation that fought apartheid. But one of the big problems is that many of the PAC leaders did not, and still don't, write their own histories."

The role played by many of the white people who opposed apartheid has also been largely forgotten. They include people such as Father Trevor Huddleston, who spent years in the vanguard of the anti-apartheid struggle ministering to people in the townships of Johannesburg and who was eventually recalled by his church amid fears for his safety; Mike Terry, who led the British Anti-Apartheid Movement for more than two decades; and British Labour politician Peter Hain, who grew up in South Africa and joined the AAM aged 17 after his activist parents fled into exile to avoid arrest.

Also largely forgotten are the white students of the National Union of South African Students, who took to the streets to oppose apartheid, and the thousands of young white

History is all we've got, because we do not know the future

men from the End Conscription Campaign, who chose prison or exile rather than serve in the South African Defence Force.

In his first State of the Nation address, the recently appointed president, Cyril Ramaphosa, called for all South Africans to come together for the good of South Africa.

But it remains to be seen whether, with a new president in place, they will be offered a wider sense of their own recent history. ⊗

Raymond Joseph is a veteran reporter for numerous South African newspapers. He is based in Cape Town

ABOVE: An exhibit at the Apartheid Museum, Johannesburg, which commemorates 131 opponents who were hanged under apartheid-era anti-terror laws

CREDIT: Jaime Saldarriaga/Reuters

Colombia's new history test

47(01): 60/63 | DOI: 10.1177/0306422018770120

As Colombians head to the polls this spring, **Irene Caselli** asks how they can determine their country's future without knowing its past and whether a new law making history compulsory is set to change that

WHEN COLOMBIANS HEAD to the polls to vote for their new president on 27 May – the first presidential election since the signing of the historic peace agreement in 2016 – they will also be choosing a version of their country's history. On the ballot is a former Marxist guerrilla fighter; the chief negotiator for the government in the peace accords; a former Bogota mayor, who some fear is aligned with Venezuela's Nicolás Maduro; and a candidate who was fiercely against the peace talks.

At the same time, a commission within Colombia's Ministry of Education will be grappling with a complex endeavour: how to teach the history of Latin America's longest-running conflict, one that has, over five decades, seen the Colombian state and paramilitary organisations pitted against anti-government rebel groups.

The debate over how the conflict and the peace agreements will be taught to young people has been making headlines over the past months, following a bill that re-established the compulsory teaching of Colombian history in primary and secondary schools.

The new bill, which came into effect in December 2017, reversed a 1994 law which had taken history classes off school curriculums, making them part of a wider social sciences module together with geography, anthropology and politics.

"The absence of this subject in the curricula of Colombian schools has led to a sort of amnesia or historic and cultural illiteracy," said Viviane Morales, a former senator – now running for president – who proposed the new law.

"The government promoted a whole generation of young people who do not know their origin and are not clear about the root causes of the conflicts we are experiencing today."

The approval of the law was initially welcomed by academics and educators.

"It is absurd not to have a history class in a country that needs to reflect constantly on conflict," said Ana María Otero-Cleves,

assistant professor of history at the Universidad de los Andes in Bogota. "The citizens' possibility to exercise their rights depends on a minimum knowledge of the country's history."

But how to implement the new law has been controversial.

While Morales was adamant that a new history class would be introduced in schools, the Ministry of Education said this was not the case.

"History has always been taught in schools. If you establish an independent class, you take history out of context," Mónica Ramirez, director of quality at the Ministry of Education, told Index on Censorship.

She stressed that the law's objective was to strengthen the teaching of history in connection with other subjects and to update teach-

The absence of this subject in the curricula of Colombian schools has led to a sort of amnesia

ing methods, but not to have history taught as its own subject.

"What makes the difference in this law is that the focus is on the history of Colombia," she said.

The ministry's effort will be led by a commission composed of educators and historians, who will have until June 2020 to launch a new curriculum.

"It is true that Colombian history is taught superficially. But having a new document is not going to guarantee that this is going to change," said Nancy Palacios, a specialist in curriculum and social studies education at Universidad de los Andes. "The most important thing is to follow up with teachers, give them training."

Teaching history in Colombia is a daunting task. It is estimated that some eight million Colombians have been victims →

→ of the armed conflict over five decades, including forced displacement, homicide, disappearance, torture and kidnapping. As a result, society has become deeply divided between victims and perpetrators, creating different readings of the same incidents, and a highly polarised political scenario.

Moreover, several regions are still experiencing armed violence, and many elements

Teachers said they could not teach about the conflict because their students were involved with armed groups

are volatile. For example, the peace deal with the Revolutionary Armed Forces of Colombia (Farc) rebel group that won President Manuel Santos a Nobel Peace Prize may be at risk until the signing of a peace deal with the National Liberation Army (ELN). The talks between the government and the ELN were on hold for six weeks because of violence, but are due to resume shortly.

"I think it is fundamental to teach about what happened in the country, to teach about the victims and re-establish emotional ties. To me it is a moral duty," said María Andrea Rocha, educational co-ordinator at the National Centre of Historical Memory (CNMH), a government-led centre to promote dialogue and memory surrounding the armed conflict.

The CNMH has led workshops with teachers and students across the country, which resulted in the development of a set of books to help teachers approach the subject of memory. In one case – in the war-torn region of Chocó, on the Pacific coast – teachers said they could not teach about the conflict because their students were involved with armed groups and it could put everybody's life at risk. So they came up with a different

kind of exercise. Students had to make an album of their lives, recreating the moment of their birth, collecting the items that could bring them back to their childhood and interviewing relatives. "The objective was to highlight the value of life in a place where life can be thrown away easily," said Rocha.

In another project dealing with memory in a creative manner, the teacher Arturo Charria asked students to tell a story of the armed conflict that was close to them through an object. Charria remembers that the father of a student thanked him because the project had given his family the chance to talk about a painful kidnapping that had happened years before. "When a topic handled in class makes it to the dinner table, something is happening inside the student," Charria told Index.

But these are isolated attempts.

"At school, the focus was on how to pass an exam, on the grades, not on understanding

PUTTING BOLÍVAR ON THE MAP

IRENE CASELLI writes about how one man has come to dominate Venezuela. It's not who you think

Hugo Chávez, who ruled over Venezuela for 14 years until his death in 2013, became known for imposing his own view of history on the country. He adopted Simón Bolívar as his spiritual father and called his left-wing movement after the South American 19th century independence hero. Chávez saw parallels between El Libertador's efforts to free South America from the Spanish conquistadores, and his own crusade to challenge US influence in the region.

Chávez was so fascinated by Bolívar that

the political and social context in which we live," said Daniela Diaz, a 21-year-old history student. "I would say that school did not prepare me for a political life."

But can this new law give young Colombians a chance to dig deeper, and to be better prepared to face their new political choices? Most remain sceptical.

"This history law can be an opportunity, but not necessarily a solution," said Rocha. "If we go back to traditional history, to memorising dates, heroes, to an elitist view of history, that does not solve anything."

"With the current polarisation, it is important to understand," said Otero-Cleves. "History gives you a chance to see the shades of grey. This is why it is so urgent that young people see this from a young age." ⊗

Irene Caselli is a journalist, who has spent the last decade reporting from Latin America

ABOVE: Farc election poster in Bogota, Colombia, January 2018

he exhumed his bones in 2010. He wanted to prove that the Venezuelan enlightened aristocrat had not died of tuberculosis in 1830, but had instead been murdered. While the DNA tests proved inconclusive, Chávez unveiled a 3D image of Bolívar based on the exhumed bones.

In the name of his hero, Chávez tweaked many national symbols. The country was renamed the Bolivarian Republic of Venezuela, and Congress changed the Venezuelan flag and coat of arms. The new design added an eighth star to Venezuela's yellow, blue and red flag, in line with the will of Bolívar, who had counted eight Venezuelan provinces that had rebelled from Spain.

Schools were not spared. Chávez, who increased public spending on education, launched a Bolivarian school curriculum, to leave behind what he called a colonial and euro-centric education model that promoted consumerism.

A textbook introduced in 2011, which was free but not compulsory, was dedicated exclusively to Bolívar.

It compared his ideas and scripts to the new constitution approved in 1999. It wrote: "Many of Bolívar's proposals go beyond the time in which he lived. Your task, and that of our entire youth, is to get to know his ideas, value them, and put them into practice in your social, ethical, political and cultural behaviour."

The tradition did not change after Chávez's death. His successor, Nicolás Maduro, has been widely criticised for promoting a cult of the late president (and in so doing of Bolívar). In 2015, the dates of Chávez's birth and death were added as historical dates into textbooks, and they were declared school holidays.

Breaking from the chains of the past

47(01): 64/66 I DOI: 10.1177/0306422018770121

Colonial governments in the Caribbean tried to destroy damning historical sources. Historians today still struggle to recapture the details of the past, writes **Audra Diptee**

THERE'S A BATTLE going on over Caribbean history. Not only have the historical documents of the Caribbean been mostly written by the white colonists who dominated the islands – with all their biases, self-interests and concerns – but there was a systematic attempt by those in power towards the end of colonial rule in the mid-20th century to destroy any records that might incriminate them. This has left Caribbean historians today with far fewer sources from which to work, and made it much more difficult to piece together what happened.

It was a Machiavellian scheme of epic proportions. The British Colonial Office implemented a programme called Operation Legacy, which ran from the 1950s until the 1970s. As countries became independent, its goal was to destroy systematically any colonial records that might be considered an embarrassment to the British government.

Instructions were given for incriminating documents to be burnt to ashes or put in weighted containers, which were to be dropped far from the Caribbean shoreline. Those that were not destroyed were "migrated" to Britain, where they not only remained inaccessible, but their very existence was denied. Only in 2011 did the government admit that the Foreign and Commonwealth Office was holding 8,800 files from 37 former colonies.

Although the term Operation Legacy was only coined in 1962, colonial records were being destroyed before. Take the case of British Guiana. Among the several thousand files that were secretly held by the FCO, none could be found that dealt with the colony. This was despite the fact that the British played an instrumental role in overthrowing the democratically elected People's Progressive Party in 1953, had a strong security presence throughout the 1950s and there was a covert but aggressive series of bombings executed in collaboration with the USA during the early 1960s, notes the historian Richard Drayton.

In the context of the Cold War, any colony with political parties that espoused leftist ideologies was not only a concern, but a reason to act to prevent them. Operation Legacy was put in place to remove the evidence of any such action.

During the 1960s, instructions to remove official documents were also given in Trinidad, Jamaica, as well as the Leeward and Windward Islands. In at least one memorandum produced by the Commonwealth

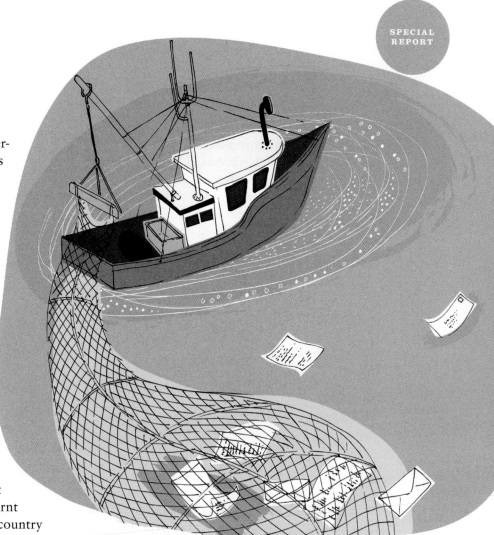

Office, it was stated in no uncertain terms that "it has always been British policy to withdraw or destroy certain sensitive records prior to independence," according to journalist and author of the book The History Thieves, Ian Cobain.

Education curriculums have been another arena used by various colonial governments to control historical narratives.

Cynthia McLeod, a well-known Surinamese novelist who specialises in historical fiction, told the History Watch Project that under colonialism, "we hardly learnt anything in school. Suriname was not important enough. We only learnt that Suriname was a backward country [and] that nothing of Suriname had any value. The less you spoke about Suriname the better ... Of course, there was Surinamese history but seen from the Dutch perspective. We never learnt anything from the Surinamese perspective. Never."

The situation was the same for the British, French, Spanish and Danish Caribbean, which saw the imposition of history curriculums developed in Europe. In fact, in Guadeloupe, Martinique and French Guiana – former colonies of France which never gained political independence and now have French departmental status – the decisions about the history curriculum, in both primary and secondary school, continue to be made by the Ministry of National Education in France.

When some colonies became independent nations during the 1960s and 1970s, new history curriculums were devised to serve a new purpose, one that was in opposition to that which existed under colonialism. Young Caribbean nationals were taught history

that celebrated Caribbean people who challenged colonial rule, fought against racism and contributed to the making of their nation. In 1979 the very first secondary school examination in

The education system was being transformed from one that imposed colonial state memories into one that imposed national state memories

Caribbean history was offered by the Caribbean Examination Council throughout the English-speaking Caribbean. The education system was being transformed from one that imposed colonial state memories into one that imposed national state memories.

The battle for the historical consciousness of Caribbean people has taken place in public spaces too. Increasingly, under →

→ national governments, there have been efforts to establish sites of commemoration that are in line with state-sanctioned national histories. Jamaica has dedicated monuments to individuals from the 18th and 19th centuries who fought against the system of enslavement, such as Sam Sharpe and Nanny of the Maroons, as well as anti-colonialists. In Guadeloupe, despite its status as a department of France, there are still streets called Rue du Nègre-Sans-Peur (road of the black without fear) and Place des esclaves (square of the slaves).

In 2017 there were calls to rename Milner Hall at the University of the West Indies in Trinidad. It was named after Lord Alfred Milner, who played an instrumental role in setting the stage for South African apartheid. This February it was renamed Freedom Hall.

He had no doubts that how Caribbean people understood their past would influence how they engaged with their present

In Fort-de-France, the capital of Martinique, a marble statue of Joséphine de Beauharnais (the first wife of Napoleon Bonaparte) still stands in La Savane Park, but it has no head. It was removed by unknown individuals in 1991, and the statue is vandalised to this day with red paint to symbolise the blood at her beheading.

"For over four and a half centuries the West Indies have been the pawns of Europe and America," wrote Eric Williams. As both a historian and a Caribbean politician, he had no doubts that how Caribbean people understood their past would influence how they engaged with their present and how they imagined their future. He wrote the first national history of Trinidad and Tobago in 1962 "to provide the people … on their Independence Day with a National History"

which would act as an "essential guide to their future action" and place "their problems at all times in international perspective". There was an urgency, he believed, to replace colonial histories with national ones.

Locating sources that provide the perspective of the Caribbean lower classes continues to be a challenge for Caribbean historians, but they do exist. There may be few written records that give them voice, but historians have learnt much from archaeological studies, as well as folklorists and anthropologists who collected or documented "cultural texts" such as stories, songs and rituals.

Nor have politicians or professional historians had a monopoly on historical narratives.

In much of the Caribbean, music has been a cultural space in which alternative histories are told. In Haiti, for example, there is a strong tradition of using popular songs performed in Creole that speak to both history and politics. Historical fiction has also played an important role in subverting conventional historical narratives. For her historical novel on Elisabeth Sampson, the wealthiest black woman in 18th century Suriname, Cynthia McLeod told the History Watch Project that she did extensive research in numerous archives.

"Her name features in all the history volumes," she said. The assumption was always that she became the mistress of a white man and inherited her wealth. There was a need "to correct that". All the evidence shows that by using her entrepreneurial talent it was she who "made white families rich".

In the war over the historical imagination of the Caribbean, McLeod has struck a damaging blow. The battle for the Caribbean past continues to be a battle for the Caribbean future. ⊗

Audra Diptee is an academic, author and managing director of the History Watch Project, an organisation that brings together activist scholars. She grew up in Trinidad and Tobago

Rebels show royal streak

47(01): 67/69 I DOI: 10.1177/0306422018770122

When protesters went out on the streets in cities across Iran, some of them were calling the name of the former shah. But are they really calling for a return to the past? **Layli Foroudi** reports

IN MOST OF the protests that rose up in more than 80 cities and towns in Iran earlier this year, people were there to rally against something. For some it was the price of eggs, for others it was corruption. Sections of the crowds were protesting against the government's interventions abroad, others objected to the mandatory hijab. There were, however, a few small gatherings across the country who seemed to be calling for something. They were shouting the name Reza Pahlavi, the would-be heir to the abolished Pahlavi throne, who hasn't been to Iran since he was a teenager, when his family was deposed by the 1979 revolution.

Most of the young people who were also chanting "Reza Shah, rest in peace!" – in reference to the first shah of the Pahlavi dynasty – and "A country with no shah has no order" would not have been alive under the last shah of Iran, Mohammad Reza Shah.

Some would even be the children of dissidents imprisoned by the shah or revolutionaries who worked to overthrow him, so the burst of Pahlavi pride among Iranian youth was surprising. Do they really see returning to the past as progress?

What the protesters were calling for in a concrete sense isn't clear. However, the fact that the Pahlavis featured at all in these protests is an indication that popular memory of that period is not dictated purely by textbooks and official accounts (from which details of the shah and his reign have been removed).

The protests sparked a social media storm of comparisons among Persian speakers, questioning whether life in Iran had improved or worsened in the 39 years since the revolution.

The Instagram posts and tweets started off by pointing out the relative losses, such as a stronger economy and social freedoms; then other users got involved to counterbalance, tweeting out the regime's achievements, such as national elections and the rise in literacy rates.

One post that circulated was of two images placed side by side: a photo of a group of women in a park, all wearing the hijab, next to a retro shot of women sitting, reading and wearing short skirts, with their heads uncovered. An opposing post showed a picture of the shah kissing the hand of the former Queen of Denmark beside a photo of Ayatollah Khamanei working alongside farmers with the caption "We gave humiliation and got dignity".

"It's reflective of the way that popular history takes hold," said Ali Ansari, professor of history at the University of St Andrews, in Scotland. "In the last 30 years, because of →

CREDIT: Monica Almeida/Reuters

→ greater literacy in Iran, because of social media, mass media and others, people are taking control of the history they want to read."

In particular, Ansari points to the television channel Manoto, which broadcasts from London and is watched by up to 70% of Iran's population.

"Manoto has produced these documentaries on the shah and Reza Shah and people are watching them avidly," he said. "They're great propaganda, actually – very well made. It seems to me that has been absorbed."

For Mahsa, a postgraduate student at the School of Oriental and African Studies, in London, her history class in Iran was a means to an exam grade, not an education. "Most students know that the history is totally biased – everyone expects it to be biased – but they are just accepting it, reading it and taking the exam," said the 26-year-old,

who moved to London from Iran last year. She said the gaps in her knowledge were filled by the internet, her parents and Manoto.

But nostalgia – of which there is plenty in Iran – induces a kind of historical revisionism. On the Manoto show Time Tunnel, viewers are teleported back to an Iran that allowed women to wear short skirts and where citizens could drink and dance, without mention of the less palatable aspects, such as the lack of political freedom, extreme inequality and the torture carried out by the shah's secret police force, the SAVAK.

The photos of uncovered smiling women are also decontextualised and say nothing about the women who wanted to wear the hijab but had their veils forcibly removed by police officers under Reza Shah's Kashf-e hijab (removal of the veil) policy.

On social media, Manoto and a host of

diaspora satellite channels that broadcast out of Los Angeles, Iranians who are dissatisfied with their present find a rosy and mythical past to look back on.

"The vibe and aesthetic [of Manoto] is chic and beautiful," said Shervin Malekzadeh, a scholar on the Middle East at the University of Pennsylvania.

"They present in a seemingly objective fashion. The programmes are not overly sentimental, but are done in a way to reassure or remind people that life was better prior to the revolution."

The Islamic regime's official narrative of the Pahlavi period tries to do the opposite. In this history, said Ansari, the Pahlavis are "nothing but Western stooges, bought by the British or by the Americans depending on which coup you want to look at".

Like Mohammad Reza Shah before him, Ayatollah Khomeini cared a lot about history and controlled how it was told. After the overthrow of the shah, the revolutionary government kickstarted a publishing drive that launched hundreds of academic journals, including more than 70 history titles.

Khomeini was specific about how he wanted the shah's downfall and the revolution to be framed, writing in a note to a historian: "You must show how the people struggled against tyranny, and the oppression of stagnation and backwardness."

To ensure a smooth rewriting period, university campuses were deserted by state decree between 1980 and 1983 and thousands of academics and students were either not allowed to return or left the country. This left a lot of archival material and history publications in the hands of the government, such as the journal Tarikh-e Moaser-e Iran (Contemporary Iranian History), which was overseen by the ministry of intelligence.

Negative nuggets of Pahlavi trivia became a valuable commodity in this publishing industry. "Officials are writing their memoirs and they struggle to get through any positive commentary about [Mohammed Reza] Shah,"

said Ansari. "One of the ways of getting published in Iran is to have an element of slagging off the shah – [for example], he's a tyrant or a womaniser. There has to be something to show just what a floozie he was."

Shayan, a BBC journalist who does not write using his surname, lived in Iran until he was 20 and remembers how his history class framed the infrastructure projects that were built under Reza Shah.

"Most of Iran's major roads were built under him; the rail network – everyone knows about these projects because they could see them," he said. "What was interesting was that they were justifying that he didn't do these things because he was a patriot – [they said] he did those things because he wanted to pave the way for British business to pour in."

But Shayan, who monitored the protests for the BBC, doesn't think that people actually want the monarchy to be restored. He sees the pro-shah slogans as "a reaction to all the propaganda they've been fed over the years".

Malekzadeh doesn't see the pro-monarchy

Because of social media, mass media and others, people are taking control of the history they want to read

murmurs as a real call for regime change, either. "Lots of kids wear the symbols of Zoroastrian practice as an expression of defiance," he said, referring to the ancient Persian religion that has also become of nostalgic cultural interest in Iran. "But that doesn't mean they'll be attending services at the temple any time soon."

Perhaps the pro-monarchy protesters are just part of the against something crowd after all. ⊗

Layli Foroudi is a freelance journalist based in London

OPPOSITE: Protesters wave the image of Iran's deposed shah Mohammed Reza Pahlavi at a rally calling for more freedom in Iran, held in Los Angeles

Checking the history bubble

47(01): 70/71 | DOI: 10.1177/0306422018770123

The historians of the 21st century have to sift through social media to verify their sources, but it can be complicated by attempts to spin the facts, says **Mark Frary**

THE IDEA THAT history is written by the victors is compelling, but one that looks to be on increasingly shaky ground in a world where a growing number of people form their views, and others influence news (and historians), from within the bubble of social media.

The rise of social media means that analysts and historians trying to understand the outcomes of conflict now have access to more primary sources, on all sides, than ever before.

The quote about winners being the ones to write history – frequently attributed to Winston Churchill, almost certainly erroneously – no longer rings true. Social media-users are trying to write the rough draft of history all day, every day.

In today's world, people get their news and analysis of conflicts in real-time from Twitter, blogs and Facebook Live. This coverage of conflicts – a far cry from the days of delayed

postal despatches from war correspondents in far-flung corners of the world – means that public opinion can be influenced on a global scale almost immediately. In the same way that 24-hour TV news influenced opinions of the Iraq War, social media is also affecting how conflicts are viewed. What is considered history may be highly dependent on what media sources are used, and those that use multiple sources for their news are likely to get a truer version of the facts.

The problem for historians analysing and trying to source the "truth" at arm's length is that users of social media are likely to have their beliefs about an event, a battle or a change of government underpinned by seeing only similar content that supports their view from within the social-media bubble.

"Whether a claim (either substantiated or not) is accepted by an individual is strongly influenced by social norms and by the claim's coherence with the individual's belief system – ie, confirmation bias," wrote Michela Del Vicario in one study, published by the National Academy of Sciences of the United States of America.

Knowing this, actors in conflicts are pressing social media into service as propaganda tools.

Peter Hough, associate professor of international relations at the University of Middlesex, said that social media is being widely used by governments to put their own spin on events, leaving historians to try to sort the spin from the reality.

"As an example, the Russian government made extensive use of Twitter to deny their military presence in Ukraine and portray the government in Kiev as neo-Nazis," he said.

Damian Radcliffe, professor of journalism at the University of Oregon and a fellow of the Tow Center for Digital Journalism at Columbia University, said: "Separating fact from fiction, intent to deceive versus human error, will only become more important as social news consumption – and news gathering – continues to grow."

The ability of social media to influence opinion and enable history to be written "on the fly" means that regimes are deliberately blocking, either temporarily or permanently, distribution networks.

Turkish president Recep Tayyip Erdogan ordered the shutdown of Twitter, Facebook, WhatsApp and YouTube in Turkey in the aftermath of the unrest there in 2016, for example. The BBC and other media now routinely solicit stories via chat apps and Twitter and the eyewitness accounts gathered through these channels regularly appear in their output.

What has remained the same is that revisionism always takes place through the filter

Actors in conflicts are pressing social media into service as propaganda tools

of the mores of the time when the later history is written.

And there are still concerns about whose version of history you should believe, said Hough.

"Social media helps good, independent historians by helping them expose falsehoods and establish the facts [but] it gives an unprecedented platform for poor historians peddling post-truth fantasies and conspiracy theories."

The challenge for historians is that they are now required to make their analysis faster than ever before (often on news channels) and in full view of the public, who have already used social media as their news channel.

So it is no surprise that states and other combatants are keen to exert their influence over the historians attempting to record events of today and yesterday.

To paraphrase US jazz poet Gil Scott Heron, the revolution will not be televised, but will be live-tweeted, snapped and posted. ⊗

Mark Frary is a journalist and author

Franco's ghosts

47(01): 72/73 | DOI: 10.1177/0306422018770124

A new Spanish movement is trying to find more than 100,000 missing victims of General Franco's regime, writes **Silvia Nortes**

"**N**O ONE WANTED to fight, no one wanted any clashes. The civil war was still vivid in the minds of the oldest generations." Sofía Navarro, now 71, is recalling the transition from General Francisco Franco's Spain. She said the dictatorship generated a society unable to think independently. "And that apathy towards politics can still be seen today."

Forty years ago, Spain emerged from Franco's regime, beginning reconciliation between the two sides from the civil war of the 1930s, the pro-Franco side and the Republicans. Reconciliation did not include coming to terms with the past, however, which was largely buried.

"The Spanish transition process was designed as a revolving door for the dictatorship," said Emilio Silva, president of the Association for the Recovery of Historical Memory, which is spearheading a new social movement that seeks greater historical enquiry and justice. "Two big policies were put into motion by the state: erasing crimes and producing ignorance."

Criminals were hidden, according to Silva, and documents were destroyed. "If it wasn't for this new social movement, the war generation would have died in silence, and we would have been left without memory."

Fedor Adsuar Casado, himself imprisoned during Franco's time, said: "History is being told too late".

"A lot of victims have died without telling their experiences to their children or grandchildren. I have even met people who learned in the '90s that his or her father was imprisoned during the war, because no one had told them before. Not even their mothers."

One key area for the new movement to address is the whereabouts of more than 114,000 missing people. This process has been stalled by convoluted legal proceedings.

In Cobertelada, in the province of Soria, for example, six teachers were killed by Franco's troops in 1936. Their bodies were buried by local farmers. It was recently agreed that a local court would take charge of the exhumation works. But in June 2017, proceedings were dismissed and the families had to proceed through crowdfunding.

"I feel a huge anxiety… It's been eight years now since we started with the investigation and the searching," a relative of one of the victims said in the newspaper Público.

Some progress towards recognising the victims of the regime had already been made. In 2007, Spanish lawmakers approved the Historical Memory Law, intended to recognise – and broaden the rights of – those who suffered under Franco. Children and grandchildren of people who were forced to flee from Spain were given Spanish nationality, and Republican files and documents – even films – were recovered.

As for the missing dead, there are certainly signs of change, said Silva. "I am receiving requests from students who are

CREDIT: Susana Vera/Reuters

researching mass graves. A few years ago, this was unthinkable."

But progress is slow. "The saddest thing is that there are a lot of people that will not live to see an effective change happening," Silva said.

Worse still, when Spain's ruling People's Party won its landslide majority in 2011, the allocation of funds for the implementation of the Historical Memory Law was cut by 60%. Then, in 2013, its funding was entirely cut from the national budget.

Enrique Díez, a professor at the University of León, has researched how the civil war and the dictatorship is presented in schools. The study analyses the latest editions of 21 textbooks commonly used. The results show dominance of a simplistic narrative, which makes both sides accountable. Maintaining this neutrality means silence on topics such as the repression of the Republicans, including the 104 concentration camps that were documented between 1936 and 1939.

Díez said that when filming the documentary The Silence Fields, looking at the experiences of Republican prisoners in concentration camps, he found many students from a school in the León region were not aware of these camps.

"Some of their grandfathers had even been held prisoners in these camps and worked as slaves ... in coal extraction. The students had not been told about their grandparents being victims of systematic repression, and did not know some of these camps were located in their own village," recalled Díez. "When we visited the site and explained to them what happened there, they felt deeply moved because a huge part of their own story had been hidden from them."

There's also silence on the role of the Spanish Catholic church, which supported Franco's uprising and took part in repression during the dictatorship by, for instance, reporting Republican families to the authorities. Díez argued that silence was partly because of the church's many links to publishers, editors

and the ministry of education.

According to Díez's study, just 44.4% of textbooks used in high schools talk about the systematic repression under Franco.

This historical bias cuts both ways, said Juan Pelegrín, who has been teaching history for almost 40 years. "Teachers coming from a Republican family are very likely to focus on repression and victims, whereas teachers coming from pro-Franco families are not."

Secondary school student Alba Cánovas learnt about the darker sides of Spain's past only because "my grandfather and father lived through it and remember quite a lot of anecdotes". She said her family education differs from education at school.

"People my age don't show special interest in this part of Spain's history and don't talk about it outside the classroom, so it should be given more importance in schools."

Cánovas counts herself lucky for getting this education at home. At a family level, Franco's legacy has more typically left a mark of silence. "Fear is still alive in the oldest generations," said Díez. ⊗

Silvia Nortes is a freelance journalist based in Murcia, Spain

ABOVE: A woman protests lack of justice for her father and uncle (pictured), who were executed during Franco's regime, Madrid 2013

Standing together

GLOBAL VIEW

47(01): 74/75 I DOI: 10.1177/0306422018770125

Protecting free speech means supporting those you don't like as much as those you do, writes **Jodie Ginsberg**

THIRTY YEARS AGO this spring, a series of strikes began in Poland that helped mark the beginning of the end of communist rule in the country. The strikes were sparked by a wave of repression by the government against activists in the Solidarity trade-union movement.

Earlier this year, I had the great privilege to spend time at the European Solidarity Centre in Gdansk, the birthplace of this astonishing movement. It was a chance to reflect on the way in which Solidarity drew together individuals from widely different industries and social strata who came together initially in support of striking ship workers and then recognised the power of that solidarity to achieve much greater change.

Recent movements such as #MeToo remind us of the continued importance of solidarity, but I worry that in many other cases we have forgotten the lessons taught by movements such as Solidarity in standing together – despite political or social differences – in support of a common principle. As Solidarity co-founder and former Polish president Lech Walesa observed: "The thing that lies at the foundation of positive change, the way I see it, is service to a fellow human being."

An event held at the museum during my trip to Gdansk reminded me of this. I watched as representatives from different journalist unions discussed media freedom.

As journalists from one group complained that they were being sidelined by new laws that gave increasing power to the new conservative Polish government, a conservative journalist hit back. "Where were you," she asked, "when we were being shut out of the corridors of power? Where were your arguments about media freedom then?"

The point she makes is one often heard, too, in Turkey, where journalists now facing arrest and detention are accused of having failed to speak out vociferously enough when their colleagues on the other side of the political divide were being hounded under previous regimes.

It is not enough for us to stand for a principle only when it suits our political ambitions. If certain universal principles – such as the principle of media freedom or freedom of expression – are to be upheld, they must be defended even when those under threat are not those "on our side". Acting in solidarity is what gives movements strength and individuals the strength to carry on: it is harder to hit many targets than one.

Index recognised this in 2015 when we called for all those who believed in freedom of expression to stand together to show their support for Charlie Hebdo, the French satirical magazine whose employees were murdered for having satirised Islam.

"We believe that only through solidarity

– in showing that we truly defend all those who exercise their right to speak freely – can we defeat those who would use violence to silence free speech," Index wrote in its call for simultaneous publications of Charlie Hebdo cartoons by other rights groups and media journalists.

Without such solidarity, those fighting to speak freely are alone – and vulnerable.

Matthew Caruana Galizia, the son of murdered Maltese journalist Daphne Caruana Galizia, who is himself a journalist, speaks passionately about the importance of standing in solidarity.

"We have to let journalists in that position [of being harassed into censoring a story] know that they don't have to self-censor; that within the international community of states and organisations, they have allies who will give them the backing that they need," he told the Gdansk conference in February.

He described how one Polish journalist at the conference had defended Poland's new Holocaust law. "Members of the audience chose to speak out against this outrage instead of remaining silent. Now we must tell Polish journalists that when the censorship law comes into force three months from today, it is their duty to break it, and that the international community will back them in doing so."

Having someone's back is easy when it's a friend, or someone whose worldview accords with our own, but much more challenging when that person seems to sit in the enemy's camp.

Former charity boss Kate Gross, who died from colon cancer aged just 36, captured this brilliantly in her blog The Nuisance, which later formed the basis of her book Late Fragments.

"I wonder if compassion has to be practised," she mused. "It is a muscle in our body, there from birth in all of us except the most

LEFT: Solidarity leader Lech Walesa being carried during a strike in Poland, 1980

psychopathic monsters. But it needs to be exercised; I can't let it sit flabby and loose like my tattered abdominals and just expect it to suddenly power-lift weights. No, this muscle needs a regular workout."

Acts of solidarity provide that workout: speaking out on behalf of the journalist whose views you abhor when her rights are

It is not enough for us to stand for a principle only when it suits our political ambitions

being shredded; or in defence of the artist whose work you despise when he faces the censor's axe; or in support of the politician whose opinions veer from your own when she faces jail. These are the acts that force us to put compassion into practice. In so doing, we act not just in service of our fellow human beings, as Walesa identified, but in service of humanity. ⊗

Jodie Ginsberg is chief executive of Index on Censorship. She tweets @jodieginsberg

IN FOCUS

MAIN: Performers in a cabaret in 1930s Germany

How gags can remove gags

47(01): 78/80 I DOI: 10.1177/0306422018769575

Heard the one about the comedian who walks into a Palestinian refugee camp to promote free speech? **Tracey Bagshaw** discovers from **Mark Thomas** that the punchline is not always as expected

"**IN THE REHEARSAL** room, nothing was off-limits. Once on the stage it became more problematic," recounts Mark Thomas, who is as well-known for his work as a free speech activist as he is for making people laugh.

The comedian and journalist was walking the barrier between Israel and the West Bank when he first came across the Jenin Freedom Theatre in 2009.

"It was a theatre. In a refugee camp," he said. "All my buttons were pressed. Here is something that exists in the face of adversity. It's the toughest place – and here's a theatre in the middle of it. What that speaks of is human beings and their aspirations – the need to express themselves and the urgency to do that – and that's thrilling. I was bowled over."

The theatre stands in a camp on the outskirts of Jenin, founded to house displaced Palestinians fleeing or expelled from Haifa when Israel was created in 1948.

The theatre itself was founded in 2006 as a place for children and young people to express themselves freely. However, many in the camp and the city disagree with the theatre's very existence, and since its inception in 2006 the theatre has been firebombed, its performers have been threatened and (half-Palestinian, half-Israeli) director Juliano Mer-Khamis was murdered right outside in 2011.

With its controversial performances – its version of Animal Farm ended with the characters in the final scene dressed as Arabs and Jews – which mix male and female actors on stage, it is a place where performers and the audience risk their lives

CREDIT: Lesley Martin

just to get through the doors.

Although its radical performances are partly what sparked the backlash, much of the prejudice came down to basic beliefs that men and women should not share the same stage. Thomas recounted the story of one actor who was escorted to the theatre by her family to protect her from those who thought she had no place being there.

"This was a theatre people were fighting to get in," said Thomas. "I was captivated and inspired. I found it thrilling."

It was this inspiration that gave Thomas

Its version of Animal Farm ended with the characters in the final scene dressed as Arabs and Jews

the idea of setting up workshops in stand-up, which he calls "the ultimate form of freedom of expression".

"The thing with stand-up is, we can say what [other] people can't say. When you're improvising, the thought barely touches the sides of your head. It's out there before →

ABOVE: Mark Thomas outside Jenin Freedom Theatre; OPPOSITE: Mark Thomas, Faisal Abu Alhayjaa and Alaa Shehada rehearsing together

→ anyone can do anything about it. It's the ultimate form of freedom of expression. But how do you do that in an area which has a whole range of social, military and political constraints that tell you what you can and can't do?"

These voices weren't often heard – it's a generational shift. It's becoming more liberal

The answer was "just do it anyway".

And, in spite of the backlash against women performing at the theatre, four women took part in Thomas' workshops, and young women made up the bulk of the audiences for the performances.

Thomas remembers one young woman's act, which poked fun at the rules laid down for women.

"She would talk about things people would find mundane, like about getting a

ABOVE: Children watching a performance at the Jenin Freedom Theatre, in a refugee camp in the Palestinian city of Jenin

boyfriend and the rules her dad had – who she could see, who she couldn't..." said Thomas. "She finished up by saying: 'We can't see boys, we can't hang around with boys, maybe we should just see women'. "

Religion was generally a no-no, but Yasser Arafat was a topic up for discussion. "He's the Pope of Palestine," joked Thomas. "You could make jokes about him. You had to be careful, but you could."

Jokes were also made about the intifada, the occupation, corruption and everyday life.

One of the comedians had a most unique routine – recognising the sounds of different types of gunfire in the camp.

"Just everyday things..." mused Thomas.

But there are signs of change in the camp. Many people from Jenin have travelled, worked away and come back, bringing with them new ideas and attitudes, which are cutting through the more traditional conservatism.

"These voices weren't often heard – it's a generational shift. It's becoming more liberal. More alert. More questioning," said Thomas.

He believes the next chapters of Palestinian history will be written in places such as this. And Thomas himself is now touring his comedy show Showtime from the Frontline, telling the story of the theatre around the world. Two Palestinian comedians from the club – Faisal Abualheja and Alaa Shehada – are performing alongside him.

Thomas hopes one day to take it back to Jenin, "maybe with a few tweaks".

Until then the Freedom Theatre will carry on, its stand-up comedians will continue to get the message out, fighting gender stereotypes, gunfire and firebombs with belly laughs. ⊗

Mark Thomas is on a UK tour with Showtime from the Frontline until April 21. More on: www.markthomasinfo.co.uk

Tracey Bagshaw is a freelance writer and editor based in Norfolk, England

Behind our silence

47(01): 81/83 I DOI: 10.1177/0306422018769576

Refugees try not to speak out of turn, wary of upsetting people in their new homelands, **Laura Silvia Battaglia** reports from Italy

"**THE SIX MONTHS** in prison in Libya were terrible. I will say no more," said Radwan, 30, who was born in Sana'a and was one of 21 Yemenis transported to Italy via the first national humanitarian corridor in December last year. "A Libyan television channel even broadcast the news of a group of Yemenis being arrested by the Libyan police in Tripoli: it was us. I keep that video on my mobile phone, but with a sense of shame: my family does not know, and must not know, anything about it."

Self-censorship by asylum-seekers often starts with the psychological shock of finding what awaits them in places they thought would be safe, and in order to avoid the shame of having to recount the unspeakable.

Radwan and his roommates in Bergamo, Italy, are wary of recounting the reasons they came to the country, and of explaining why Italy is not their desired destination. Fathi Mohammad mentions a fiancée in the Netherlands and said he'd like to join her there.

"Many asylum-seekers self-censor their stories, at least until their first meeting with the Territorial Commission, which will decide whether or not to grant permission," explained Michele Spadaro, a lawyer working on refugee asylum requests in Italy.

Riad Kadrawi has been a Syrian refugee in Italy since 2014. He is one of those who has made it. He obtained asylum, and today teaches Arabic and works with refugees and asylum-seekers. He is from Ghouta, where part of his family still lives. "I am considered by many people to be the perfect refugee: I learnt Italian quickly, I began working after obtaining asylum," he said.

"But I have censored myself many times, especially about what happened to my family members in Syria. We Syrian refugees in Italy come from many realities and have differing pasts. I am always afraid that there may have been other Syrians in the reception centres who were spying on me."

Kadrawi's fear of being spied on is rooted in stories that have circulated amongst →

BELOW: People from the Kurdish community protest in Rome against the Russian and Turkish bombing of a Kurdish area of Syria, January 2018

→ refugees in Turkey, Greece and Italy about supporters of Syria's President Bashar al-Assad infiltrating their communities. In Turkey, for example, there were allegations that a former member of the Turkish intelligence services abducted a former Syrian military officer from a camp and sent him

There may have been other Syrians in the reception centres who were spying on me

back to Syria, where he was reportedly executed. In other parts of Europe, there are rumours of informants collecting information, informing secret services and punishing relatives still in Syria.

For Kadrawi, being the "perfect refugee" can come at a cost. He feels pressure to change his habits and assimilate, starting

with not praying five times a day. Still, when it comes to his free speech, he appreciates that in Italy he can be critical about the authorities without it leading to his arrest or torture. Recently, when some members of his family were killed in Ghouta, Kadrawi was outspoken in his condemnation of the attacks.

"I feel freer now to say what I think of Assad, but I also feel like someone without a homeland: I do not belong anywhere, in fact. Or perhaps I belong only to some middle land which is mainly inside myself," said Kadrawi, weighing up the pros and cons of his current situation.

Amin Wahidi, 36, arrived in Italy in 2007, obtaining political asylum within a year. He is from Afghanistan and is a Hazara. Back home, he was a television anchorman at ATN. "One of my female colleagues, an ethnic Hazara, Shaima Rezayee, who worked at Tolo TV, was killed by the Taliban. They also wanted to kill me," he said.

what you have experienced. And you prefer to keep quiet."

Wahidi knows that feeling able to speak freely doesn't apply to everyone. "There are people who leave the path of free expression altogether, even if they were artists or intellectuals before, because there are people for whom it is enough just to get out of difficulty. I have learnt that for many people it is enough just to feel alive," he said of those who might be so relieved to be away from danger that they don't want to rock the boat.

Wahidi is currently working on a film called Milestone, which tells the story of an Italian street singer, Manuela Pellegatta, who lives in Milan. Wahidi's move away from ref-

LEFT: Migrants arrive in Augusta, Italy, June 2016

I feel freer now to say what I think of Assad, but I also feel like someone without a homeland

Wahidi, who was a screenwriter in his own country and had founded a production company, fled Afghanistan after beginning to shoot a film, The Key to Paradise, about a potential suicide bomber. In Italy, he began all over again, spending time at the cinema school in Milan and producing four short films, as well as Behind Venice Luxury, the story of a Hazara refugee in Italy.

"One's original identity and one's new identity rebalance themselves only after many years," he said. "My heart is still in Afghanistan, but Italy has given me freedom of expression and has enabled me to be reborn as a director.

"Art has enabled me to stop censoring myself, but what I can testify is that it has not been easy. At the beginning, when you arrive in Europe from a distant world, you are in shock from what you have been through. And self-censorship is a necessary rite of passage. In fact, if you talk, you don't even know whether people will understand

ugee stories and those concerning his country of birth is partly because he fears that production companies will change his story or force him to deliver different messages. He had a bad experience with a US production in Afghanistan, when he felt he was being used to get across a certain message.

Herein lies the flipside of the censorship story. It's not just what refugees feel they cannot say or have to hold back. It's also what they feel forced to say, feeding into certain narratives which are often politically motivated. In this instance, Wahidi said he was not willing to do so because "I don't sell myself to anyone". ⊗

Some last names have been left out for security reasons

*Translated by **Sue Copeland***

Laura Silvia Battaglia *is an Index contributing editor who reports from Yemen, Iraq and Italy*

Something wicked this way comes

47(01): 84/87 I DOI: 10.1177/0306422018769577

Songs banned by the Nazis will be performed on the London stage this summer. **Abigail Frymann Rouch** interviews Dame Edna Everage's alter ego, **Barry Humphries**, about his involvement

RECORD PRODUCER MICHAEL Haas arrived at work one day to find a large cardboard box on his desk. Inside was sheet music written by obscure inter-war German and Austrian composers, and a message from the sender – signed: Barry Humphries. At the time (the early 1990s), Haas had no idea of Humphries's lilac-haired alter ego, Dame Edna Everage, who had been seducing and shocking television audiences for many years with her razor-sharp wit.

"I had him down as an erudite, serious music collector," recalled Haas.

Humphries, now 84, has been fascinated by inter-war German and Austrian music since boyhood, his curiosity piqued by music he found in a second-hand bookshop in Melbourne in the 1960s.

In his suburban surroundings, Humphries said that, as a boy, he saw Jewish refugees arriving from Europe and had heard of the horrific experiences they experienced. "You might say I empathised with them," he told Index. "They were a hell of a lot more interesting than the average Australian."

What Humphries had sent Haas was music by composers who the Nazis had sought to silence. After Adolf Hitler came to power in 1933, the Nazis shut down cabarets and banned artists deemed unacceptable. In doing so, they slammed the door on a dazzling, but ephemeral, period of artistic creativity and political and social boundary-pushing.

Germany's Weimar Republic, then blamed for many of the devastated country's ills, had given new and radical ideas space to flourish.

In the cabaret bars of 1920s Berlin, *chanteuses* (female singers) – wearing just a thong, or dressed as men – sang about women's rights, lesbianism and abortion. Men in the 1920 Lavender Song, by Mischa Spoliansky and Kurt Schwabach, proclaimed: "We're not afraid to be queer and different." Capitalism, anti-Semitism, gender roles and German notions of racial "degeneracy" were thrown into the crucible of cabaret to be challenged, mocked and reimagined.

RIGHT: Liza Minnelli as Sally Bowles in the film Cabaret, set in Weimar Germany

Did they appeal to Humphries's mischievous side? "Yes," he chuckled in response.

In the 1970s, Humphries met Spoliansky, who had fled to London and gone on to write film music for the Rank Organisation. "I looked him up because I wanted him to write a song for Dame Edna," he said. But the project didn't mature. "I told him the kind of song I wanted and I sang it to him and he said, 'I couldn't do better than that', which was very complimentary."

Having brought a selection of the songs back to the stage with cabaret singer Meow Meow in London in 2016, Humphries is preparing for three weeks of performances of his Weimar Cabaret at London's Barbican this July. One of his favourites is a duet about escape called Benares, by Kurt Weill and Bertolt Brecht from 1927.

"It is a desperate, beautiful song on the dilemma that would soon confront so many people in Europe," he said.

Its pleading phrases make for uncomfortable listening because of our knowledge of what would follow. And even the more upbeat songs carry a foreboding that the good times would not last.

The Nazis had clear views on what made for wholesome music and what made for music it termed "degenerate". Acceptable music was German or Austrian (Hitler adored Wagner, Beethoven and Bruckner) and not Jewish. "Degenerate" included styles considered foreign: US jazz, which they called "nigger music", avant-garde atonality, and, of course, anything written or performed by Jews or people of Jewish heritage. It could include classical music as well as cabaret.

In 1938, an exhibition starkly called Entartete Musik (Degenerate Music) opened to enable the public to experience, and be suitably disgusted by, such works. (The more famous exhibition of "degenerate art", of which Humphries is also a defiantly keen collector, was held the year before.) A promotional image for the music exhibition shows a black saxophonist depicted as

It is a desperate, beautiful song on the dilemma that would soon confront so many people in Europe

a monkey, wearing the Star of David and a gypsy earring. It parodied a poster for a provocative, jazz-influenced opera Jonny Spielt Auf! (Jonny Strikes Up) by the Austrian composer Ernst Krenek.

Finding their works exhibited signalled the beginning of the end for artists in Nazi Germany or Austria, if they had not already fled. Jewish and communist performers, songwriters and composers found themselves barred from the stage or having to leave their jobs. Many fled to France, Britain or across the Atlantic. Krenek fled to the USA in 1938 after years of harassment by the regime. Others who did not manage to leave Europe – such as singer and film director Kurt Gerron, who had performed opposite Marlene Dietrich – died in concentration camps.

Krenek's music was among the second-hand manuscripts Humphries stumbled →

ABOVE: Barry Humphries performs music from Germany's Weimar Republic with cabaret singer Meow Meow at the Edinburgh International Festival, 2016

→ across, along with works by Kurt Weill, most famous for the Threepenny Opera; Erich Korngold, who turned to writing film scores for Hollywood; and avant-garde composer Wilhelm Grosz, who died on reaching New York in 1939, aged only 45. Humphries, presenting a Sky Arts documentary last year, said: "The art and the music of a country before disaster strikes takes on a kind of intensity, a glow, a radiance."

A key figure in reviving this musical legacy is, of course, Haas, who has researched the composers and works banned by the Nazis, and publicised many of them by making recordings. Haas has been a music curator at Vienna's Jewish Museum and co-founded Vienna's Exil.arte centre, a repository for the music estates of exiled composers. He said that while some music and related documentation was lost, much was hidden in plain sight, poorly archived by institutions that lack the language skills to get to grips with

Had I been around then, I would have been sent away

it. "Hostlands," (as opposed to homelands), he explained, "often only took what was relevant to them, and that was often the least important part of their output."

European exiles had to adapt to the Hollywood tastes of their new employers and abandon the edgier styles they had been crafting.

Today, younger artists are discovering and interpreting these works for a new generation. Peter Brathwaite, a black baritone who performed a programme of Entartete Musik in 2014, was shocked by the lyrics' rawness. While he was performing Weill's Song of the Brown Islands, which uses grotesque racial stereotypes, he said it hit home that "I am the black man, singing this!", and he found himself shaking on stage.

"Had I been around then, I would have been sent away. I wouldn't have been able to

perform or collaborate with other artists," he told Index in an interview at London's RSA.

Separated by a generation, the performers approach the songs differently. Humphries, along with Meow Meow, argued that "the defiant mood of these artists and composers is called for" because "we're living now in an age of a new Puritanism, of betrayal, of people telling on each other; of absurd political correctness carried to ridiculous extremes."

In May, Brathwaite will perform a show

COMPOSING THE RIGHT NOTES

A new book on Shostakovich looks at the composer's ability to transcend the worst abuses of Stalinist terror. DANYAAL YASIN talks to the author

"Music has a profound effect on people, and that is not something dictators tend to like," said Stephen Johnson, BBC music broadcaster and author of How Shostakovich Changed My Mind. The book, published this April, explores the power of Dmitri Shostakovich's music during Joseph Stalin's reign of terror.

Like other composers in the Soviet Union, Shostakovich's music was judged first and foremost on its political values, and he had to tread a fine line between what was acceptable and what was not.

His musical career was defined by the harsh censorship he faced under Stalin, described as a "personal terror campaign" by Johnson. The composer himself once said that life in Stalin's regime was "unbelievably mean and hard".

Stalin didn't just censor music. He used it as a tool to control the masses and help further his ideology.

"During the siege of Leningrad, many people were removed; Shostakovich wasn't," named Effigies of Wickedness at London's intimate Gate Theatre in collaboration with the English National Opera, alongside mezzo-soprano Katie Bray and a consciously diverse line-up of artists. The show's artistic director, Ellen McDougall, believes some communities still suffer exclusion by "invisible structures" such as gender-binary language. Gay rights have taken a step back, thanks to "a swing to the right" in the USA, Europe, Russia and Ukraine, she told Index.

And women's rights, access to abortion, the links between war and capitalism, and over-reliance on oil are as much issues today as when the songs were written.

Will today's listeners give the Weimar cabaret songs, with their warnings of imminent destruction, a different reception, I asked McDougall. "I live in hope," she said. ⊗

Abigail Frymann Rouch is a freelance journalist, based in London

INSET: Dmitri Shostakovich photographed in Germany, 1950

---

said Johnson. "I think this was partly because he was such a valuable cultural exhibit in a way, because he was popular abroad and useful as a propaganda tool. They wanted him there, but on their terms."

Despite the restrictions, artists such as Shostakovich managed to hide their rebellions in plain sight. Arguably his most famous piece, his Symphony No. 7, also known as the Leningrad Symphony, is an example of how his music spoke volumes across the country and around the world. His longest piece, lasting 75 minutes, it demands an enormous amount of stamina from its performers. Viewed by those in the West and the Soviet Union as a rallying cry of the Russian people during the war, it had a double meaning for the composer.

Performed while Leningrad (now St Petersburg) was under siege by Nazi forces, it was outwardly a piece against the city's invaders, but Shostakovich also used it to subtly attack Stalin's brutality.

Stalin simply saw the symphony as a tool for the Soviet Union's propaganda machine. Performed in the Grand Hall of the Leningrad Philharmonia, it was broadcast by loudspeakers across the city in August 1942.

The usefulness of Shostakovich, however, was limited.

"I wouldn't say Stalin liked people, but if he thought they were a good thing, he would play horrible cat and mouse games with them,"

said Johnson. Shostakovich fell foul of Stalin in 1948, denounced for "formalism" and "Western influences", after which most of his music was banned. The denunciation hit the composer hard.

In today's climate, his work is not played nearly as much in Russia as it is in the West, according to Johnson.

"Perhaps he's a bit uncomfortable for people out there. I think maybe he's talking about things a lot of people don't want to be reminded of," the author said.

"He can still make people feel uncomfortable. I really think he can. That's something else that's marvellous about his music. He can still speak to people in power and cause discomfort."

Danyaal Yasin is the editorial assistant at Index

Fake news: the global silencer

47(01): 88/91 I DOI: 10.1177/0306422018769578

"Fake news" has taken off around the world, with political leaders using the catchphrase to plant mistrust in the media, stop stories being published, and even imprison journalists, reports **Caroline Lees**

PRESIDENT RODRIGO DUTERTE of the Philippines accuses journalists of reporting "bullshit"; Tanzanian president, John Magufuli, has imposed a new law policing social media for "false and misleading information"; President Andrzej Duda of Poland says "false reports" by journalists are undermining democracy and the rule of law. All three are planning to take measures to censor independent media for what they describe as press "inaccuracies".

"Fake news", the favourite way for US President Donald Trump to insult critical journalism, has become an international political catchphrase. Over the past year more than 20 political leaders worldwide, from authoritarian regimes to European democracies, have used the term to accuse reporters of spreading lies as a way to discredit journalism they do not like. These accusations are being used to justify the closure of critical news outlets, to imprison reporters, to censor content and to block public access to the internet and social media sites.

Jean-Paul Marthoz, author, academic and veteran journalist, believes the attacks are strategic and deliberate, intended to weaken opposition voices and, in particular, legacy media.

"The labelling of prestigious media as 'fake news' outlets by those who are the major emitters of fake news is part of a determined attack against the system of checks and balances which define and protect liberal democracy," he said.

The fake news message reflects current populist anti-elite and anti-establishment sentiment, according to Marthoz, who said: "Many rulers believe the approach taken by Trump surfs on the relatively widespread unpopularity of the media among the public they target with their populist or nationalist messages.

Over the past year, political leaders in Burma, Cambodia, China, Egypt, France, Germany, Hong Kong, Hungary, Kuwait, Libya, Malaysia, the Philippines, Poland, Russia, Singapore, Somalia, Syria, Tanzania, Thailand, Turkey, the USA and Venezuela have publicly accused journalists of reporting, or being, fake news.

Approaches differ between countries, but there is evidence such attacks on media credibility are becoming more widespread. The latest annual prison census released by the Committee to Protect Journalists reveals a sharp increase in the number of journalists imprisoned on false news charges.

At least 21 are in jail worldwide, in at least six countries. Last year there were →

RIGHT: People protest in Kansas City, USA, to demand an investigation into President Trump's constitutional conflicts and ethics violations, 2017

CREDIT: Brian Cahn/Rex

just nine journalists jailed on such charges, in two countries. The trend of using fake news as an accusation has taken off globally.

In the Philippines, Duterte has been waging a very public war on particular media outlets, often labelling them "bullshit" and "fake news". The latest target is Rappler.com, the country's only digital-born news site. In January this year, the government announced it would revoke Rappler's operating licence.

The day after the announcement, Duterte described Rappler as a "fake news outlet" that published stories "rife with innuendos and pregnant with falsity."

He added: "Since you are a fake news outlet, then I am not surprised that your articles are also fake."

Rappler's founder and editor, Maria Ressa, is fighting back. She accuses Duterte's government of systematically spreading fake news itself, to "silence and intimidate" opposition.

Courtney Radsch, CPJ's advocacy director, monitors such attacks on the press. She predicts the term "fake news" will continue to be used against the media in authoritarian regimes, and expects more states to adopt statutes against it.

"I would anticipate that countries that lack democratic safeguards and robust press would be happy to use this as an excuse to restrict journalism," she said.

In Tanzania, four independent newspapers and two radio stations have been shut down or suspended over the past 12 months because of what President Magufuli has deemed to be "inaccurate" reporting. Most recently, Daima – a newspaper that had previously criticised the government – was closed for 90 days last October after being accused of spreading "false information".

The president's moves against the press follow the introduction of a controversial cybercrime law in 2015, which prohibits the publication of "false and misleading information". It has already led to the arrest of eight opposition party workers for sharing "inaccurate" election results over the messaging service WhatsApp.

Similar measures, ostensibly implemented to stop the spread of fake news, are being taken elsewhere in Africa. During the recent elections in Somaliland, all social media platforms were shut down on the grounds they could spread "inciteful and tribalistic information, in the form of hate speech and fake news".

Melody Patry, advocacy director for Access Now, a non-governmental organisation campaigning against internet shutdowns, said a number of African countries have used a "kill switch" to block either the internet or individual social media platforms during elections and protests. These countries include Cameroon, Ethiopia and the Democratic Republic of the Congo.

"Using a kill switch to cut off communications is a blunt-force instrument resulting in suppressing free speech and denying access to information," Patry said.

The instrument used against the media in some European countries is more subtle. Hungary's government recently announced that, while it supported press freedom, it would not tolerate any outlets considered to be "spreading fake news, misleading the public and limiting the people's access to real information". Since coming to power in 2010, the country's prime minister, Viktor Orban, has been criticised for repressing press freedom. Respected independent media outlets have become openly pro-government after being acquired by Orban's political allies. One, Hungary's leading opposition newspaper, Népszabadság, was closed down in 2016.

Poland's ruling Law and Justice Party (PiS) is also increasing control over the country's media and regularly uses the platform provided by pro-government media to attack the credibility of independent outlets. Recently, during a live news programme on public channel TVP Info, a government minister criticised a respected online news site, Gazeta.pl, calling it "deceitful, shameful and the worst thing on the internet".

The site is owned by Poland's first private independent newspaper, Gazeta Wyborcza, which has been accused by PiS of being an "enemy of the state".

Attempts to prohibit "disinformation" and "fake news" in liberal democracies have also come under scrutiny. French President Emmanuel Macron plans to allow authorities to block content or close down sites deemed to be spreading "fake news" during election periods.

"When media organs spread slanderous falsehoods, they are no longer journalists," he said.

But others questioned whether governments should have the right to decide whether a piece of news is fake. In February this year, Macron himself was criticised for allegedly influencing a decision to sack the head of Radio France. He had previously been accused by Macron of spreading "false rumours" about their relationship.

Efforts to undermine trust in independent media is having an impact on audiences, according to Liz Corbin, editor of Reality Check, the BBC's fact-checking team.

She said: "Seeds of doubt are being sown and that is incredibly dangerous for the future of the free press."

Trust in the media has significantly declined over the past decade, according to the Reuters Institute for the Study of Journalism. A 2017 RISJ report – Bias, Bullshit and Lies, Audience Perspectives on Low Trust in the Media – cites a US Gallup poll showing media trust dropping from half (53%) in 1997 to less than a third (32%) in 2016. There has as yet been little evidence to show how far "fake news" claims have directly contributed to the decline, but the RISJ study identifies the way politicians and bloggers use social media to publicly question the motivations of journalists and news organisations as one factor affecting trust.

Another recent poll, asking Americans if they understood the meaning of "fake news", revealed some public awareness of how the term has become politicised. Nearly half (47%) of respondents said it referred to "sloppy or biased reporting", while 39% described it as an "insult being over-used to discredit news stories people do not like".

Seeds of doubt are being sown and that is incredibly dangerous for the future of the free press

Marthoz predicts authoritarian governments will continue to deliberately undermine trust in the media. He believes public awareness of the issue is one of the few ways to resist what has become a global threat to media freedom. Legislating against the flow of disinformation is impossible, he said, and it is also undesirable if it means abusive control and government censorship.

But public awareness is unlikely to make much difference in authoritarian regimes around the world, where reporters have been arrested, news outlets have been closed down and journalists censor their own work for fear they will be accused of lying. ⊗

Caroline Lees is a former Sunday Times correspondent in Afghanistan, and now works for the Reuters Institute for the Study of Journalism at Oxford University

LEFT: Maria Ressa, CEO of online news outlet Rappler, is interviewed at a protest against the outlet's licence being revoked by Duterte's administration, Manila, Philippines, January 2018

CREDIT: Lynn Bo Bo /Rex

The muzzled truth

47(01): 92/95 | DOI: 10.1177/0306422018769579

Democratic transition in south-east Asia hasn't brought the region's journalists the freedom it once promised. Some journalists are trying to navigate censorship, while others are leaving the profession, writes **Michael Vatikiotis**

discovery of a mass grave and had been given some classified documents by police officers. They were arrested almost immediately, and later charged in court under a colonial-era Official Secrets Act. The elected government of Burma, led by Aung San Suu Kyi, was unmoved by the global outcry for their release.

Even more chilling was the impact the arrests had on local journalists, who have seen their expectations of media freedom greatly undermined since 2015's general elections, including the use of criminal charges to curb critical reporting.

"More and more of them are choosing to look for other jobs," said a former journalist who has been training local reporters in Burma.

Even more chilling was the impact the arrests had on local journalists

Across south-east Asia, journalism is currently facing a broad range of challenges, from physical threats to life and intimidation, to prosecution, usually under arcane laws of sedition and defamation. But none is more insidious than the self-imposed censorship many working journalists adopt in order to survive.

For the many years I worked as a correspondent for international and regional publications in the region, I encountered all kinds of intimidation: there were phone calls from high officials to editors; attempts at bribery in the form of cash in envelopes; and the ever-present threat of prosecution under harsh laws that usually have their origins in the colonial era.

Malaysia, for example, uses stringent laws of sedition and an official secrets act that have roots in British colonial legislation. A Canadian colleague, Murray Hiebert, spent a month in prison in →

LEFT: Journalists Wa Lone and Kyaw Soe Oo are escorted out of court in Yangon, Burma, after their first trial, January 2018

THE SCENE OUTSIDE the courthouse in Yangon, Burma in early January this year was heart-rending: two young Burmese journalists working for Reuters were brought to court in handcuffs after spending a month in detention without charge or access to their families. One of them cried when he saw his young wife and daughter.

Wa Lone and Kyaw Soe Oo had been reporting on south-east Asia's biggest humanitarian crisis: the forced exodus of more than 650,000 Muslim Rohingya from the Buddhist majority Rakhine State.

They were working on a story about the

→ Malaysia for contempt of court. "I lost my freedom, which is a rather shocking thing to have happen, for writing about a debating team," Hiebert later told The New York Times. Hiebert had written about the wife of a Malaysian judge who sued a school for dropping her son from the debating team, with a comment on how unusually quickly the case came to court.

Many of us simply don't believe we can fight the system, so we just do what we can

That there are not legions of reporters in prison speaks of the practical way most working journalists deal with the problem, which is either to find ways of reporting the truth which skirt the law, or not to report the truth about sensitive issues at all.

As one young Malaysian reporter put it to me recently: "Many of us simply don't believe we can fight the system, so we just do what we can, pocket our wages, and hope for better times."

There are those who choose to fight. Wa Lone and Kyaw Soe Oo defiantly told the media outside the court room in January that they were being persecuted because they were reporting the truth. They face minimum jail sentences of 14 years.

But there are many who simply adapt to survive. This mostly means that sensitive topics are avoided, but they can still be broached.

For example, there is a long tradition of using oblique and indirect writing techniques to skirt draconian press laws in south-east Asia. Ambiguity and avoidance is possible in cultures and languages in which obliqueness is both acceptable and meaningful. Reporting in another language, such as English, has also helped to get things around government watchdogs.

As a correspondent for, and later as editor of, the Hong Kong-based Far Eastern Economic Review, I worked for more than two decades spanning a period of rapid economic growth and political change. The review was staffed by a collection of foreign reporters, mostly long-time Asia hands, as well as courageous local journalists who often put their freedom on the line to report on current events.

The review was hounded and punished by governments for its brave liberal stance on the politics of the region. In 1987, the Singapore government took the magazine to court after disputing the veracity of what transpired in a meeting between Prime Minister Lee Kuan Yew and the Catholic archbishop of Singapore. The review lost the case, was fined and had its circulation severely restricted in what was then one of the magazine's largest markets.

Yet, for all the legal battles, intimidation and incarceration, we got away with a lot, although there was inevitably some self-imposed restraint driven by the need to keep reporting. I found that by deploying the tools of empathy and understanding I could say much more. This did not mean I wasn't telling the story, but the amount of detail I was given licence to use allowed me to offer explanations and different points of view.

Also, when you had the luxury of writing at length on a weekly basis, you could play the long game and write indirectly. There were ways to articulate the shameless monopoly former President Muhammad Suharto's children maintained in key areas of Indonesia's economy, simply by delving in detail into the ownership structure. There were ways to comment on Malaysian Prime Minister Mahathir Mohamad's iron grip on power and refusal to tolerate dissent, simply by offering a blow-by-blow account of how he wielded power and dealt with the victims.

The review closed as a weekly publication in 2004, due to a funding decision made by its US proprietors, Dow Jones. I still live, work and write from the region, and although I no longer work as a reporter, I still have a keen sense of the new challenges facing journalists today.

In the age of the internet and social media, it is no longer so easy to be indirect. There is little room for subtlety in 280 characters. With reporting in the English language so much more common online, laws apply just as much to what is reported in English as they do in Thai or Malay or Chinese. Before, governments could simply ban publications. Today, they cannot afford to switch off the internet.

The plight of reporters in Thailand and Malaysia is particularly acute because of the refurbishment and strengthening of laws that carry prison penalties for expression in the spoken or written word: the Official Secrets Acts 1972, the Sedition Act 1948 and – the granddaddy of them all – the Printing Presses and Publications Act 1984.

Although the Printing Presses and Publications Act has been amended so licences for press and permits for publications no longer have to be renewed annually, licences can be revoked at any time.

The expectation that democratic transition would liberate the media has proved misleading in many places. An established democratic government in the Philippines has not stopped 79 journalists being killed in the line of duty since 1992, according to the Committee to Protect Jouranlists at the start of 2018.

Democratic transition over the past two decades in Indonesia has seen a blossoming of media of all forms, which Indonesians have revelled in. But there are limits.

A law against insulting the president that was struck down in 2006 was reintroduced to parliament in 2015. With increasing levels of ethnic and religious intolerance, free expression must abide by more than just appropriate considerations of race and faith, and intimidation is common.

This leaves the working journalist with a stark reality: write or broadcast freely and face legal consequences. The preferred coping strategy is self-censorship.

In Thailand, reporters avoid all but the approved official news about the royal family. In Malaysia, only passing references can be made in the carefully couched language of allegation about one of the largest corruption cases in modern history involving the prime minister and his family.

There are scarcely any legal safeguards, and editors often have cautious proprietors to deal with. In the case of Singapore, the government continues to exert strict control over mainstream media expression, which jars with the comparative freedom of what can be posted on social media. A Straits Times reporter told me that his colleagues were flabbergasted when a feud between members of the prime minister's family played out openly on Facebook in mid-2017, while the newspaper was discouraged from reporting the matter.

A well-developed culture of careful omission, oblique expression and respectful criticism has evolved. In part, this sits well with the deeply ingrained culture of conflict avoidance in many south-east Asian socie-

A well-developed culture of careful omission, oblique expression and respectful criticism has evolved

ties. But, sadly, it leaves south-east Asia with media that struggles to support the efforts of civil society or opposition politicians to highlight injustice and inequality. ⊗

Michael Vatikiotis was editor of the Far Eastern Economic Review and is currently the Asia director of the Centre for Humanitarian Dialogue. He is based in Singapore and his book, Blood and Silk: Power and Conflict in Modern Southeast Asia, was published in 2017

Carving out a space for free speech

47(01): 96/97 I DOI: 10.1177/0306422018769580

Journalists pull back on coverage of controversies in Singapore, because they know what might happen to them, says **Kirsten Han**

WHEN SINGAPOREAN ACTIVISTS Roy Ngerng and Teo Soh Lung were accused of breaching election advertising laws by posting on their own Facebook pages the day before a by-election, police officers searched their homes and confiscated their electronic devices – all without the need for a warrant. Later on, other people were subjected to similar treatment.

All this was shared on social media. But there was little interest from the mainstream media. I know this because I was the only journalist waiting outside the police station for Ngerng's release that day in 2016.

There are international rankings that Singapore does care about and those that it doesn't. Press freedom is firmly in the latter category. That's why I have been involved in launching a new website, New Naratif, a platform for journalism, art, research and community-building in south-east Asia. The members of our start-up team come from diverse backgrounds, but are united in the belief that there is a need for such a project.

We are creating a space for local writers to publish their work, and also a space for stories and issues that governments and local media are reluctant to touch; where people can get informed and discuss such issues.

Singapore is wealthy and developed, its populace largely highly-educated and plugged into global networks. Yet the country is ranked 151 out of 180 in Reporters Without Borders' 2017 Press Freedom Index. As a freelance journalist focused on reporting from and on Singapore, it's not a ranking that surprises me. There are many systemic challenges in our way.

The government, dominated by the People's Action Party, has plenty of levers it controls: legislation that keeps the mainstream print and broadcast media under the government's thumb, defamation laws (and the resources to hire expensive lawyers to sue), broad contempt-of-court laws and dominance over information flows. Without any freedom of information legislation, the government releases or withholds data at will, and there is little that journalists, academics or citizens can do about it.

A reporter for The Straits Times, Singapore's main daily broadsheet, learnt this the hard way last year when she received a stern warning for breaching the Official Secrets Act after sending questions to government agencies related to a not-yet-publicised public housing initiative. She spent a night in detention while the police tried to get her to reveal her source. The person who leaked the information was fined about $1,500.

It's not easy for independent media in Singapore either. The Newspaper and Printing Presses Act, which prohibits publication unless a permit is granted by the government and gives the government the right to appoint management shareholders, essentially makes it impossible for independent media to exist in any form except online, and even that is difficult.

The authorities can arbitrarily define a website as a political association – as they did with The Online Citizen in 2011 – thus requiring it to adhere to laws on political donations, barring the site from receiving any form of foreign funding and limiting the amount of anonymous donations. An online licensing regime has also been introduced for popular websites, requiring them to put down deposits of nearly $40,000 that are forfeited if they fail to remove within 24 hours content flagged by the authorities.

But there are other challenges, too. Resources, in particular funding, are in short supply. Last year, independent news site The Middle Ground shut down after two-and-a-half years due to lack of finances.

Singapore is in crucial need of independent news sources, alternative perspectives and spaces where important yet politically sensitive questions can be asked. Challenging curbs to a press freedom requires holistic strategies and cannot be left to any one person or small group of people. Things can move forward only when there is solidarity and trust, built from ongoing conversations and the sharing of skills to organise and push for change. This is what our project New Naratif seeks to do. ⊗

Kirsten Han is a freelance journalist based in Singapore and chief editor of New Naratif, a new platform for south-east Asian journalism

ABOVE: Women on the subway in Singapore

CULTURE

IN THIS SECTION

CREDIT: Gary Waters/Ikon

Just hurting, not speaking

47(01): 100/107 I DOI: 10.1177/0306422018769581

Ahead of the publication of her new book, The Language of Kindness, award-winning novelist **Christie Watson** writes a short story tackling taboos around ageing. She talks about why to **Rachael Jolley**

COSTA FIRST **C**NOVEL award winner Christie Watson tackles taboos around health and guilt in her short story, Exit Wounds, written exclusively for Index.

Watson, a former nurse, will also publish a much-awaited non-fiction book, The Language of Kindness, next month.

In The Language of Kindness, Watson addresses not only the incredible mental and physical challenges that nursing staff face as they battle through a multitude of health crises, but also the other emotional demands such as patients with no family to care for them and mounting demands on their time.

In her short story, below, Watson uses fiction to talk about some of the same issues, telling the powerful story of an older woman, Margaret, who lives alone, and who is struggling with her health and her ability to pay for her care.

The novelist brings readers to understand how hard it is for Margaret, how alone she is and why she can't bring herself to speak about these struggles to her family.

Watson said: "Even though she is lonely, I don't think she would express it, as many older people wouldn't. We have got a real issue. The thing is that we are [all] living separately."

Watson acknowledged that, in many societies, people still found talking about death taboo. She said: "We don't talk enough about death, and it is quite a secretive process – people don't know what happens after you die. For example, when my dad died we didn't know about organising a funeral and we relied quite heavily on people who had gone through it before, but hadn't thought to ask them about the process before.

"Then it becomes a very frightening thing, because it is secretive and everything that is secretive is more frightening than the actual reality."

Watson, who lives in south London, hit the literary scene with her first novel, Tiny Sunbirds Far Away. She believes strongly that, in Britain, there are issues around ageing that are not being discussed.

"One of reasons why I love Index so much as an organisation is that it's about giving freedom of expression, giving a voice, to the voiceless. Although we have got a rising open dialogue with, particularly young,

ABOVE: Former nurse now author Christie Watson

people – [some of whom] are shouting very loudly about social issues, which is great – the one thing that still needs tackling, increasingly, is that there are a huge number of elderly people in Britain who haven't got a voice at all, who might not be able to vote, who can't see or get out, or haven't worked out how to do online voting.

"These are the people who fought for our country and who founded the NHS. We've got a big problem with, not only loneliness, but lack of voice for elderly people in our country who are almost disregarded, put to the bottom of the pile and are almost invisible.

"It's also pride. It's complicated. Not just that they are afraid or embarrassed."

She believes that there is a need for more discussion about mental health and other illnesses in arts, television and film. ⊗

Rachael Jolley is the editor of Index on Censorship

Exit Wounds

Margaret didn't like to make a fuss. But despite the number of blankets she'd wrapped around herself it was still bitterly cold. She thought about getting up and heating soup. She had a can left. Tomato. But she'd planned that for tomorrow, and then what? She wasn't really hungry. But ever so cold. And cold, when it bites you in your bones, makes you forget about hunger anyway.

Small mercies, she muttered, before turning the television up louder to drown out the silence. Jeremy Kyle. These people. Where did they find these people?

She fell asleep at some stage. Must have done, because the telephone jolted her awake. "Nan, it's me, Simon. How are you?"

She heard the great-grandchildren in the background, squealing and shouting. Imagined them. Smiled. "I'm good, love." It took a few minutes to turn down Jeremy Kyle. She liked to fill the living room with loud voices. She used to like the newspapers – felt part of something bigger – but the voices all became the same. Even the headlines. As if one person was writing for the Mirror and the Guardian and the Daily Mail. Still, at least TV had a variety of people. A man with no bottom teeth was shouting at a woman wearing a too tight vest. "How are the kids?"

"Oh we're all good, you know, busy busy, I'm just checking in. And I know we said half term we'd be down but there's a slight change of plan. It might have to wait until Easter. I've got a conference and it's really important or I wouldn't ask. I hate to cancel. We were so looking forward to visiting."

Margaret watched the Jeremy Kyle people blur in front of her. She thought of the day Simon was born and how impossibly light he'd felt in her arms. "That's OK love, I understand."

→

"Anyway, how are you, Nan? Is it cold down there? Manchester is freezing. I hope you're wrapping up warm."

"Yes, love. It's not too bad. I saw the snow you're having on the news. I expect the children are enjoying it?" She heard the voices once more, in the background.

"Stop it. I mean it – stop!" Shouting. "Come speak to Great Nan."

There was a pause. Then: "Hello grape nan."

Margaret laughed and for a few seconds there was no cold at all.

THE DISTRICT NURSE, Ellie, came on Tuesday mornings. She was ever so patient, waiting while Margaret pulled herself up onto the frame and shuffle-walked to the door to unlock it. It must have taken a full 10 minutes. "Hello Mrs Venn, how are you? Gosh it's freezing in here. Let me get the kettle on."

She was a tiny thing, a dot of a girl, can't have been much older than 20. Made a terrible cup of tea. But Margaret liked her anyway. She was much better than the first one who used to come every day before the cutbacks, the one who picked up and commented on Margaret's

---

She thought of Reg, being shot during the war, the entry wound a small, neat 50 pence piece

---

ornaments and photographs as if she and Margaret were old friends.

"Lovely cuppa for you. My goodness you're freezing. It's like a freezer in here. Have you no heating?"

"Oh I don't feel the cold, love," said Margaret. She pulled the blanket around her and stretched out her bad leg to Ellie, who was already crouched on the floor with a new dressing, wearing plastic gloves ready to take off the old.

"You know there is an emergency fund for gas and electric," she said, "if you wanted I could send an assessor out? Can't promise but still. Anyway I could come and help with the forms at least?"

"Oh no, I'm fine. Leave it to those who really need it."

"This leg isn't so good, Mrs Venn." She'd wound the bandage off to reveal a stench like rotten meat and it was twice the size of the other leg, swollen shiny redness.

"We might need to get the doctor out, but I'm not sure it will be today. And you might need to pre pay." She sighed. "I'm sorry about that."

Margaret looked down. The ulcers had grown and there was clear fluid running down them. "Chop it off," she said. "All it does is cause me trouble."

CREDIT: Alex Green

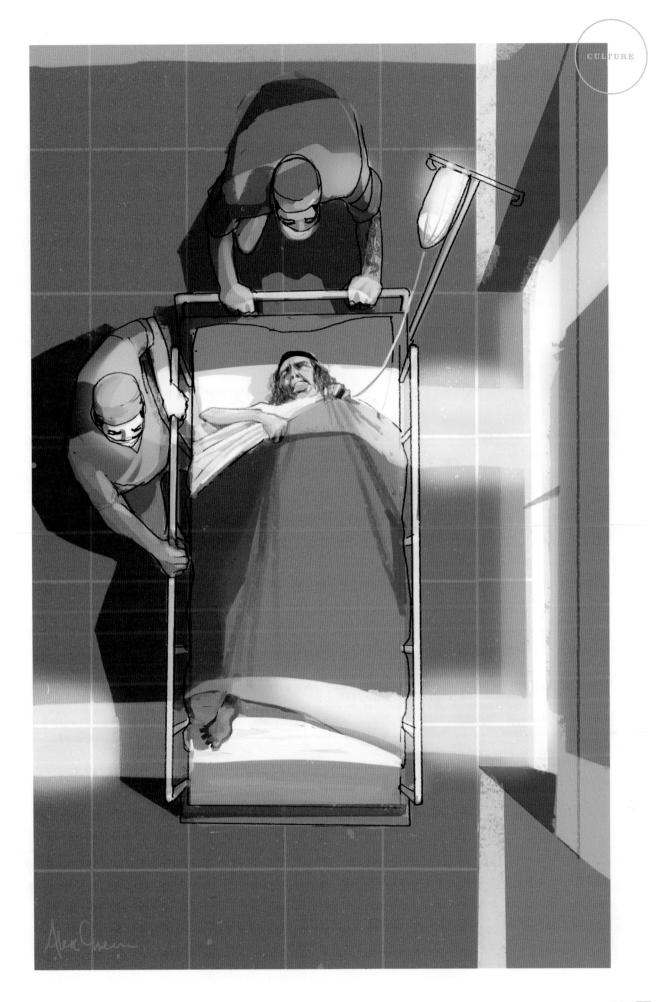

→ Ellie looked up and patted Margaret on the arm. "It'll be OK," she said. "But I do think Doctor Zadin needs to pop in. You need antibiotics."

"Don't worry, love. Anyway, I can't understand a word he says."

Ellie laughed. Folded up the stinking bandage into a bag, rolled a new one carefully around Margaret's leg. "Even so I'll ask him to come. You don't want to end up in hospital."

Margaret shook her head. She looked past Ellie, next to the TV and the small silver pot. She thought of the day they found that pot, her and her husband Reg. They'd been on holiday in Malta and walking through winding cobbled streets, lined with what he'd called "tut shops", hand in hand. Reg had a stripe of sunburn on his neck above his T-shirt. The pot that was so full now contained only seven pounds and 50 pence. A prescription 10 pounds.

MARGARET DIDN'T KNOW how long she'd been there before they came.

First was the Indian doctor shouting through the letterbox. "Mrs Venn, I can see you, stay there – help is coming."

She pressed her body into the ground. Opened her eyes. Her kitchen. The same wall clock, mug tree, spice rack. The washing-up cloth hanging over the tap. And now the can of soup on

---

She tried to call out in pain and scream but her mouth fish opened noiselessly

---

the floor, the soup splashed all up her cardigan like fresh blood. Her leg stuck out the wrong way and the pain was burning. Her head skipped back. Her mind danced across years as though time was a ballroom. She thought of Reg, being shot during the war, the entry wound a small, neat 50 pence piece, yet the exit left half his back blown off. Life was devious like that.

There was loud banging, then smashing and the door thrown open. Doctor Zadin knelt by her. "You stay still, Mrs Venn. There's an ambulance on the way." He touched the soup splashes on her cardigan. "Oh. Soup," he said. "That's a relief."

"I'm not going to hospital," Margaret whispered. But her voice sounded funny. Far away and young. Stupid. Simple. Like Patricia's voice sounded in her head. Like she was told it would be after they took her away from Margaret without letting her see. She could still hear her mother's words: "You can't keep her. You wouldn't cope with a baby at your age anyway. But a mongol? You'll have another baby. When you're married. Older. There will be others. In any case, she won't live long. Best just forget about this."

And then she was lifted onto a trolley and she tried to call out in pain and scream but →

→   her mouth fish opened noiselessly.

Her leg was fire.

She closed her eyes as they slid her trolley into the back of the ambulance. She did not want to see her neighbours watching her. Covered in soup.

"I'm Jay," a voice said. "One of the paramedics. We're taking you in to get you checked over." He put a needle into her arm. "This will help with the pain," he said, and before she could stop him, the darkness following his voice like an echo.

Lights and noise and screaming and shouting. Margaret tried to lift her head but couldn't. She felt the leg and the pain and the cold. She smelled the soup on her cardigan and sweat and heard the siren reduce to nothing.

They pushed her into the corridor and there were nurses and doctors and shouting and police around a man who was punching a wall. "Full this side," shouted a nurse wearing dark blue scrubs and a pen pushed into her ponytail. "Keep her in the ambulance or push her to the line in the corridor."

Jay smiled and held her hand. But Margaret felt her eyes flood with fear. "I need to get

---

She did not want to see her neighbours watching her. Covered in soup

---

back," he said. "I have another shout. Too many sick people are not being treated and then becoming really sick. False economy isn't it? But we're not allowed to call it privatisation. It's written in our contract." He rolled his eyes and looked down the corridor.

Margaret followed his eyes when they'd stopped rolling, down the corridor where trolleys lining the wall on which people like her were lying. Old people. Alone people.

Jay squeezed her hand. "Listen to me moaning when you're the one who's ill! I'll try and get some extra blankets Mrs Venn. You still feel cold."

She didn't want to let Jay go. She wanted Dr Zadin to come back. The man who couldn't even speak English. Imagine that. Her head flicked up the corridor where her trolley was so near the wall it grazed her elbow. What was Simon's number? There was no point phoning her son, David. What could he do from Australia? Simon's number was written next to the phone at home but anyway she didn't want him to worry either and come all that way. Wiltshire wasn't Australia but still, it might as well be. Another trolley went past them with a nurse on top of the patient pressing on his chest, another pushing the doors that swung open to public resuscitation area. Margaret glanced inside though it hurt to lift her head up. It was like a war. Something you see on TV.

Her leg was at such an angle that every time another person or trolley or wheelchair went by it brushed past it, and the fire became ice. Numb. That's when Margaret knew how bad it was. Her head flew backwards still. She was giving birth again in the barracks hospital, this time to David. Reg was outside, thinking it was her first time. The matron gave her a cloth. "Bite on it," she said. "Bear down and bite. The pain means you're alive and the baby is alive. Pain is life."

And he came out with perfectly round, non-almond shaped eyes.

She could no longer feel her leg. The wall against her arm was the only real thing. She pushed her elbow towards it until the trolley moved a fraction. Shapes of people whizzed past her. Outlines of nurses and doctors and patients and relatives. She stopped shivering. Stopped moving at all. Even her goosebumps flattened out until her skin, too, was unmoving. She ran back. Margaret was a child, at her parent's farm in the valleys drinking milk from the bottle that had a creamy layer so thick it gave her a moustache and everybody laughed. They were all in the same room. Her father was holding her mother, her uncle and aunt sitting playing

---

She didn't want to let Jay go. She wanted Dr Zadin to come back. The man who couldn't even speak English. Imagine that

---

cards at the table, their grandmother sitting on the chair singing to her cousins who were sitting by her feet:

Ni wna undyn â thi gam;
Huna'n dawel, annwyl blentyn…

And then Margaret was singing the same song to another baby. A newborn baby in her arms. A girl. Everything was dark, and softly quiet, muffled. There was no more shouting, no more fire, no screaming or police or patients or doctors. She wasn't alone any more. There was no more cold. But Margaret could see a nurse walking towards them with extra blankets. She was sure of it.

Christie Watson is a novelist and writer. Her new book The Language of Kindness: A Nurse's Story (Random House UK) is out in May

Ban and backlash create a bestseller

47(01): 108/115 | DOI: 10.1177/0306422018769582

Bestselling Palestinian author **Abbad Yahya** had to flee his country due to his latest book. **Jemimah Steinfeld** speaks to him and introduces a section from the book, translated into English for the first time

ABBAD YAHYA did not expect the publication of his fourth novel to put his life at risk. But early last year, within just a couple of months of publication, Crime in Ramallah had been banned by the Palestinian Authority. And not just banned – his books were confiscated, his distributor was detained and he received a series of death threats online. The police asked him to come in for questioning. That Yahya, now 29, was out of the country was a small mercy. But a year on, he is still living far from his friends, his family and his wife.

Crime in Ramallah narrates the lives of three men (Nour, Rauf and Wissam) caught up in the murder of a woman. Set around 2013, with flashbacks to the Second Intifada (2000-2005), it addresses the social and political changes taking place in Palestine.

The Palestinian attorney-general accused Yahya of threatening morality and public decency, and Yahya pinpoints several parts of the book that provoked the outcry. The first is when Nour discusses his teenage years and his voyage of sexual discovery. Another is a passage in which Nour is taunted by police about his homosexuality.

"I think everyone knows that these issues are open for discussion and that there is a homosexual community in Palestine, albeit in secret and within strict limitations that ensure that the discussion doesn't enter the public discourse," Yahya told Index. "What happens when these topics enter into the public sphere is that there is a violent reaction, as happened in my case with my novel."

The passage printed below also caused outrage. In it, Nour jokes that a poster of Yasser Arafat, in which he brandishes a gun, has phallic overtones. Yahya called a friend to ask if mocking the poster was worth the backlash. The friend responded: "When we all saw that image of Yasser Arafat, we thought to ourselves along the same lines as Nour did, but Nour is the only one who said it out loud."

For Yahya, "it is the duty of a novel to bring out into the open what is going on inside people's heads". Sometimes that means challenging the idea of Arafat as "beyond criticism".

He said: "I expected that the novel would be controversial. However, I didn't expect this controversy to be of such magnitude…

ABOVE: Palestinian author Abbad Yahya

This was shocking, as were the subsequent incitement and threats, which included threats to kill and physical harm."

According to Yahya, this reaction "was the first of its kind since the establishment of the [Palestinian Authority] in 1994". Certainly it was far greater than the reactions to his past books, which had themselves ruffled feathers.

"The most significant paradox," Yahya added, was that "it became apparent that subjugating freedom of expression in my case was just as violent as it was in the novel facing the characters".

Yahya, who has moved between several countries since last year, hopes to return to Palestine soon. "Ramallah is the place where I live, write in and write about," he said. If he does return, though, he will do so with trepidation, concerned that he won't be able to write in the way he used to, scared for his safety and pessimistic about the country's future.

"Things seem bleak in Palestine, whether at the political level or people's daily lives. There is a challenge which I think about constantly – namely, the reality regarding freedom of expression and creativity. I think this issue is becoming more complicated and I am concerned that many persons find themselves faced with tough alternatives," he said.

As for Crime in Ramallah, it remains banned. And yet with heightened publicity, far more people have read it than would otherwise. That his work has ricocheted beyond the traditional reading milieu is a sort of "moral compensation for the author", Yahya said, and that might be another small mercy. ⊗

Jemimah Steinfeld is deputy editor of Index on Censorship

Crime in Ramallah by Abbad Yahya

I walked away, turning my back on the throngs of students demonstrating against the "storming of al-Aqsa mosque by settlers", an event that was repeated every few weeks and was followed by the same reactions and lectures being cancelled due to pressure from angry students. I walked, my back to the students, the cries and the chanting. At the steps up to the main cafeteria, I bumped into Aya.

"Good morning," she greeted me, smiling. "How are you?"

"Good morning. I'm well, thank God," I replied coolly, kicking myself for using the word "God", a word that had somehow started infiltrating everything I said.

"There's no lecture. Everything's suspended," she declared, as if announcing the liberation of al-Aqsa.

"Yes, I went but there was no one there."

"All the lectures will probably be cancelled."

"We'll see…"

I shifted my body round to try to show that this conversation was over and that I wanted to carry on towards the cafeteria, but Aya stopped me, tucking her long hair behind one ear.

"Do you want to get something to take away, or do you want to sit in the cafeteria?" →

→ Her question caught me off guard and what surprised me even more was how different she seemed today. Or maybe it was her question that made me feel there was something different about her.

"I don't know," I replied hesitantly. "I want to see if Rauf is here or not."

"OK, have a look. And I'll wait for you here."

I nodded and walked up the stairs, thinking about how stupid my reply was, what an idiot I was, and about Rauf. Then I started thinking about how there were some words people use all the time that don't make any impact, but if the exact same words are used in a different context and particular tone, they could become the most important words of our life. I'll wait for you, Aya had said. Me, who no one ever waited for.

I started scanning the cafeteria for Rauf, as if I really had come here to look for him. Maybe I now wanted to find him so that I could get rid of this new Aya.

But I didn't find Rauf, so I bought a coffee and left, ready to face Aya, hoping that she might have gone and that she didn't really mean it when she'd said she'd wait for me. Before I reached the spot where we'd bumped into each other a few minutes ago, I thought about her. Nothing special came to mind besides the fact that she was the only one at university who had resisted the fashion of the "outer bra", as Rauf called it: that strange garment with short sleeves worn like a jacket, with ends that hung down and tied in a knot below the breasts. It was a trend that swept through the entire female student population, so much so that any girl who didn't wear something similar would stand out. And that's what we immediately noticed about Aya. This new fashion was probably a way to draw attention to their breasts and make them seem bigger and Aya didn't need that. Even now, there's nothing else that stands out about Aya in my mind other than the memory of that first summer at university.

There she was at the bottom of the staircase, looking up at the entrance to the cafeteria. Her face beamed when she saw me coming down. She tucked in some runaway strands of hair again. I stepped down and walked alongside her, convincing myself that maybe this could be a way to stop myself from thinking about Rauf.

As we walked away from the loudspeakers and the crowds of the Youth Movement and student activists and the al-Aqsa rants, I looked down at my feet and at Aya's. Aya was rabbiting on about the most important institutions and sectors that might have jobs for us once we finished at the end of term. Her chatter made me feel as if life would carry on in the same way after we graduated, and that we wouldn't need to do much to start off this next chapter of our lives on the right foot.

Aya said that what worried her most was the prospect of staying at home unemployed after graduating. I wondered if she was telling the truth or whether what she was really most worried about was graduating without being in a relationship that would lead to a comfortable marriage where she wouldn't need to worry about finding work or not. And then she'd be happy to stay at home waiting for her husband to come home from his job. →

My thoughts strayed so far that I had no idea what Aya was actually saying, as if she was talking to someone else, and tuned back in only when she asked me a question.

"What are you planning to do?"

Without thinking, I replied with an answer that hadn't crossed my mind before.

"I want to carry on studying… abroad."

My response was surprising and powerful; it silenced both Aya and myself.

We walked through the campus in silence. She looked at me and tried to say something but without any words.

"When will we see the end of all these loudspeakers and the rallies getting in the way of our classes?" she eventually blurted, after struggling to find something new to talk about. The topic was predictable; like all Palestinians, it seemed that talking about politics was a way to kill time. Then she didn't know what else to say so she started criticising the student movements. I didn't comment. My thoughts wandered to the days when it was harder to be critical

CREDIT: Mohammad Saabaneh

112
INDEXONCENSORSHIP.ORG

or candid, to my school days at the height of the Second Intifada.

There were rifles being brandished all over the place during the first year of the intifada. Demonstrations were like forests of rifles, raised high in the air by masked men who fired all their ammunition. Intermittent bursts and a drawn-out burst. The crowd surged with excitement, and uproar and chanting flooded the country.

Everyone was preoccupied with waving their rifles about and I was discovering the joys of my own little weapon. That's what I called it for a few days, inspired by the general atmosphere. Then I felt humiliated and berated myself for calling it that. The raised-up rifles remained, brandished by their owners who would show off, go wild and discharge them into the skies. And I withdrew to a remote world where I even became disgusted by my own erections, terrified of everyone and everything that stood erect.

At the time, Fatah Youth activists put up posters of their leader, Yasser Arafat, everywhere. They were plastered all over the school entrance using messy, cheap glue. On my way out of school one day, I stood looking at a poster pasted across the entire iron gate: Yasser Arafat in his military uniform standing over a heavy machine gun. Arafat was higher than everyone else in the poster and the gun was at the level of his waist. The angle the photo had been

Demonstrations were like forests of rifles, raised high in the air by masked men who fired all their ammunition

taken from made the gun look like an extension of Arafat's penis. There was a smile on his face and the other armed men in the background were staring down at their own dangling rifles, with some sidelong glances towards Arafat's erect gun, as if proof that they had all conspired in staging the photograph and that they were pleased by it, even if only secretly.

The cheap white glue was seeping out of the corners of the posters. But with the photo I was looking at, the glue was trickling out near the mouth of the rifle. The composition was perfect; the long rifle was dripping a sticky, white discharge.

The stupidest thing I ever did was to glance over at the other students who stood there looking at the photos with me, when my face said it all. Suddenly, we all burst out laughing. We laughed without having uttered a single word, but in full view of all the students leaving the school. Within minutes, a group of Fatah Youth students were darting towards us. I recognised them from afar by their clothes and the way they moved. What happened next was enough to stamp that image of them in my mind forever.

The students who had been laughing with me quickly distanced themselves from me as though singling out the one mocking the revered leader. Then our school's Fatah students →

OPPOSITE: Black-and-white images opposite and on following page are from Palestine in Black and White, a new collection bringing together 100 political cartoons by Mohammad Saabaneh (Saqi Books)

→ gathered round me and started shoving me towards the wall, speeding up as they went along, until I disappeared within this army of trousers, keffiyeh scarves, black shirts and bulky boots. No one helped me and I didn't return their punches or do anything at all to resist.

The beating died down quickly, maybe because I surrendered quickly, but then the largest guy in the group lowered his body towards me as I lay on the ground and kept trying to heave his waist at my head. He was leaning his torso backwards, shoving his crotch at my head. He thrust himself so hard at my face that his large belt buckle gashed my forehead.

It was as if he was confirming to me that my reading of the poster was accurate, that the movement's members were very capable of hitting their target and that no one was allowed to do anything about it.

Had he not done what he did in front of students who were in fits of laughter and howling, I might still be branded the boy who mocked the Old Man and his gun and accused of being unpatriotic – a heavy charge for someone of my age. But his response shifted the spotlight instead. In fact, the whole drama earned me a little bit of sympathy from those who had been targeted by a similar weapon in the school toilets, behind the school fence and in the

I disappeared within this army of trousers, keffiyeh scarves, black shirts and bulky boots

classroom at the end of the day, when the school thugs exercised their power and sexually harassed their fellow students until they made them feel like helpless little girls. I even got an interested response from some people who were curious about my submission in the face of such cruel actions.

I woke from my daydream to Aya's voice telling me that she wanted to go to Ramallah. We had reached the university's taxi rank; I hadn't paid attention to where we were walking. She asked me if I wanted to go with her. I told her that I had some things to finish off at the university. It was clear from her expression that she knew I was trying to avoid her. She left and I carried on threading through the cars and students to get a seat in any other car heading towards Ramallah. I would go to work, even if it was a few hours before my shift was due to start, since there was nothing for me to do and I wanted to finally get Rauf off my mind.

*Translated by **Nashwa Gowanlock***

***Abbad Yahya** is a Palestinian writer and editor. He has published four novels: Blonde Ramallah, Section 14, Public Telephone and Crime in Ramallah. He is shortlisted for an Index 2018 award*

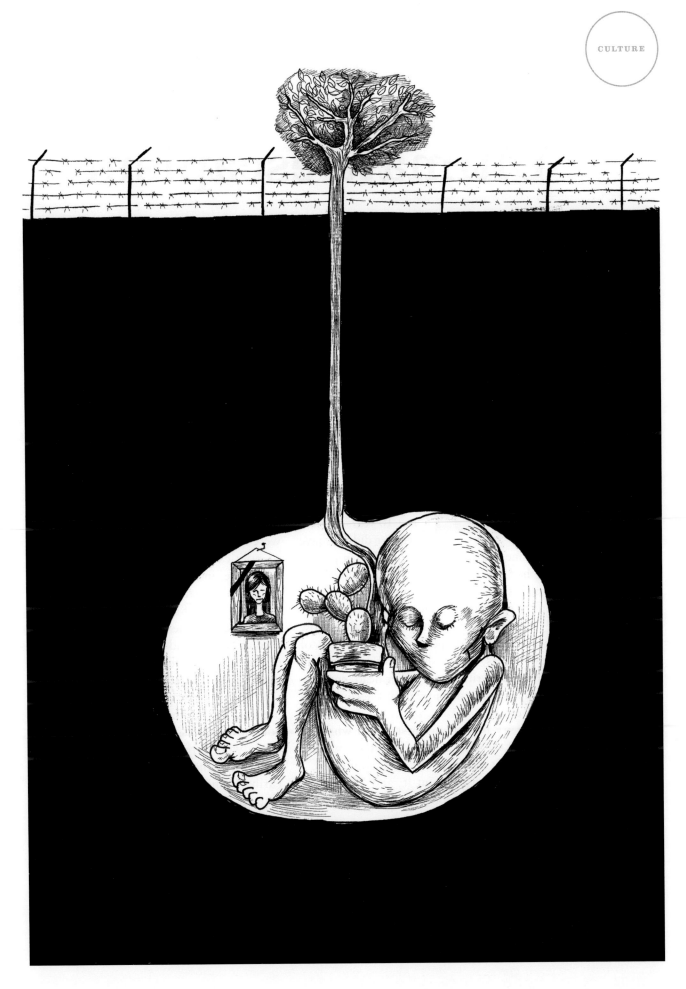

Ultimate escapism

47(01): 116/117 I DOI: 10.1177/0306422018769584

Mahvash Sabet spent a decade in an Iranian prison purely because of her faith. Recently released, she speaks to **Layli Foroudi** about overcoming religious divisions and how poetry was a survival tool

IT WAS SOLITARY confinement in a Tehran prison cell that turned Mahvash Sabet into a poet. Before her arrest 10 years ago, the teacher did not have the time or the need to write. But in prison, she had feelings of pain, loneliness and love, which she wanted to express and, with no one to speak to, she had to improvise.

In her cell in Evin prison, Sabet, now 65, began writing poems in the margins of newspapers. When she didn't have a pen, she would write verses in her head, engraining them in her memory until she could note them down.

"Poetry became my best friend whilst in prison," she said in a Skype interview with Index. "Every difficulty I encountered, I would just write about it, and I knew my thoughts [and] emotions would go beyond the prison walls."

Sent out via prison guards and during visits with relatives, the poems were published and earned Sabet the accolade of PEN International Writer of Courage in October last year.

Sabet was arrested on 5 March 2008 on a trip to Mashhad, a city in north-east Iran, because of her faith. At the time, she was a member of the Yaran-i-Iran (Friends in Iran), an informal council of seven people who supported the needs of Iran's Baha'i community, a persecuted religious minority of more than 300,000 people.

Two months later, the remaining six members were arrested in their homes and they were all subsequently convicted for a series of politically motivated charges including espionage, insulting religious sanctities and propaganda against the Islamic republic.

At the time of sentencing, Amnesty International called the trial a "parody" and the verdict "a sad and damning manifestation of the deeply-rooted discrimination against Baha'is by the Iranian authorities."

Prejudice in the courtroom translated into prejudice within the prison walls. Sabet was not allowed to associate with the other prisoners, who were told by the guards to harass her and the other female Baha'i inmate, Fariba Kamalabadi. It was even rumoured that one of the women awaiting execution had been ordered to kill them.

But this changed as they all got to know each other.

"We would not label ourselves or label others," said Sabet, whose fellow inmates were imprisoned for politics, writing, sex work and murder. "We learned to live without labels, just as human beings, side by side."

ABOVE: Award-winning poet Mahvash Sabet

There was "a feeling of commonality", she added. "I had an incredible experience from this. People that you never believed you could sit with, or eat with, or have a heart-to-heart conversation with – we would do this there."

In Sabet's mind, the divides created by the guards between her and other prisoners, and by the government between her and other Iranians, are "illusory distinctions".

In a poem of the same name, she writes:

Such frontiers, borders, boundaries of illusion!

Such barriers of fancy, distinctions of delusion!

These confines of time, these limits of space

Create unreal riddles, fences without sense.

At times, Sabet's poems intimate suffering, and she describes being undeservedly imprisoned as "a kind of agony".

Yet she wrote her poems as, above all, chronicles of love and hope. The poem published below for the first time in English was written in the penultimate year of her imprisonment and considers how a poet's heart can find strength in silence. Indeed,

her demeanour communicates no self-pity. For a woman who has spent a decade in jail, she is radiant; smiling, and with her eyes glistening, she plays with her long silver hair as she thinks.

She said that her poems were definitely read by the Iranian authorities. When I ask whether she self-censored as a result, she takes her glasses off, shakes her head, and laughs.

She describes being undeservedly imprisoned as "a kind of agony"

"The language of poetry is the language of metaphor," she said. "It helped me to write in a way that one could read it and understand the meaning, and one could also read it, but not really grasp the full meaning. I always thought 'Maybe they will come and get me', that it would create a problem for me, but I took the risk. I would pray and I would write." ✖

Layli Foroudi is a freelance journalist based in London

The word

The one who knew to speak
put a word in my mouth.
When no one had anything
  to say, even a word,
the speaker spoke and passed...
Passed...
from beyond the deserts and valleys,
from beyond the mountains and dust,
from beyond humanity,
from beyond the afflicted being
  of the half-dead world.
Now, that word is within me constantly.

In its splendour, I am bewildered.
In its power, I am agitated.
My heart is about to roar.
A word is in my mouth and
  a volcano in my soul.
Light flows from my suppressed word.

*Translated by **Rebecca Ruth Gould***

***Mahvash Sabet** is an award-winning poet and teacher from Iran*

Index around the world

47(01): 118/120 I DOI: 10.1177/0306422018769585

Attacks on journalists are escalating in areas formerly seen as safe, including the USA and the European Union, says **Danyaal Yasin**

MORE THAN 1,000 attacks on press freedom were reported in 2017 by Index's Mapping Media Freedom, the monitoring tool used to record such incidents across Europe.

Verified through a number of correspondents, partners and other sources across 42 countries, reports featured assault or injury, criminal charges and lawsuits, as well as psychological abuse and sexual harassment.

Six journalists were killed as a result of their reporting in 2017, including Daphne Caruana Galizia, a Maltese journalist known for exposing government corruption.

Her son Matthew called for other journalists to document threats made against them at the Free European Media conference in Gdansk, Poland, on 15 February 2018, encouraging them to file violations on the MMF platform.

Murdered outside her home on 16 October, when a bomb exploded under her car, Galizia's work linked many of Malta's high-ranking officials to various corruption scandals, making her the target of a number of lawsuits and threats before her death.

Also speaking at the conference was Index CEO Jodie Ginsberg. She said the mapping project was highlighted by other speakers and organisations during the conference for its importance in helping journalists.

Co-funded by the European Commission and undertaken with the European Federation of Journalists, the MMF platform has been identifying threats, violations and limitations against the media throughout Europe since 2014.

"When we started the project, it was a pilot and we could not predict, for example, that Turkey would become the place with the most journalists in jail," said Ginsberg. "The focus on Mapping Media Freedom will still be documenting threats; what we want to make sure is that we're doing it in a way in which we can deal with the increasing number of things we report.

"Because we never expected this volume of reports, we're having to make adjustments to make sure we can keep up with the amount of information that's being provided to us and keep making sure that we maintain the same degree of quality and verification."

Ginsberg also travelled to the USA on the first mission to the country by international press freedom groups, along with Index's Sean Gallagher.

Six organisations, including Article 19 and Reporters Without Borders, visited Houston, Texas, and Washington DC to speak to journalists about the changing

LEFT: Journalist
April Ryan, who
says she received
death threats over
reporting of the US
president, appears
on SiriusXM radio

nature of press freedom under the Donald Trump administration.

"I think it's clear that journalists are under a lot of pressure, and what's worrying is how normal threats against journalists have become," said Ginsberg. "Journalists talk about receiving death threats as if that was a normal part of their everyday life, and that really, really worried me."

American Urban Radio Networks White House correspondent April Ryan is one journalist who has received threats as a result of her reporting on the US presidency.

Speaking on a panel in Washington, Ryan told the crowd she and other journalists had the police on speed dial as a result.

"It's very real for some of us," she said. "For me, it's real. I've been getting death threats for asking a question, a logical question, as the press will do, and we have the right to do under the First Amendment. This is our job, we call out and ask questions.

"I'm making sure I am secure. The FBI is on speed-dial, so is the Secret Service and local police department."

Statistics from Freedom House reveal press freedom in the USA declined in the last year, reaching its lowest point in 13 years. The Committee to Protect Journalists' US Press Freedom Tracker found that at least 44

I've been getting death threats for asking a question, a logical question, as the press will do

physical attacks took place against journalists in 2017.

In awards news, the nominees for the 2018 Index on Censorship Freedom of Expression Awards have been announced.

The 16 shortlisted nominees were chosen from more than 400 crowdsourced nominations for their work in their respective →

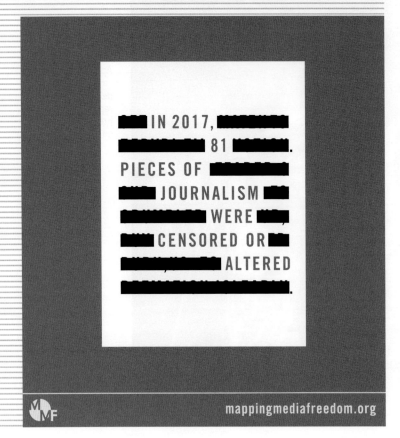

IN 2017, ████████ 81 ████. PIECES OF ████████ JOURNALISM ████ WERE ███, CENSORED OR ███ ALTERED ████████.

mappingmediafreedom.org

Freedom of Expression Awards", adding that it had come at a really important time as Russia was tightening its grip on civil society.

"Several years ago, it seemed not so dangerous to be a human rights defender or activist in Russia; we just didn't know about a lot of cases of violence towards activists before. However, today, we hear more and more news about torture by the police, people vanishing, or security services' secret prisons," he said.

"The more people know about our work, the better protected we become and the more chance we have to achieve our objectives, and to help people whose rights to information access are abused in Russia. A nomination for an international award is not only something to be proud of, but also a significant piece of support for our work."

Another nominee, in the digital activism category, is Mèdia.cat, a Catalan website devoted to highlighting media freedom violations and investigating under-reported stories. Ferran Casas, president of Grup de Periodistes Ramon Barnils (the non-profit organisation of journalists that promotes Mèdia.cat), said: "Freedom of expression is at stake in Catalonia and the Spanish state. Journalists have suffered physical aggressions, threats and other restrictions to their jobs. Some artists have been censored, and even retweeting a critical message can get you accused.

"We need to fight against this situation, unique in western Europe, and this nomination is a great encouragement to do so."

The winners will be announced on 19 April at an event in central London. Winners receive a full year of support from Index, focusing on promoting their work, building partnerships and receiving expert support in areas such as personal safety, mental health and legal protection. ⊗

Danyaal Yasin is the current Tim Hetherington/ Liverpool John Moores University fellow and editorial assistant at Index on Censorship

→ fields, covering the arts, campaigning, journalism and digital activism categories. The awards highlight those who work against heavy censorship, with many facing regular death threats and criminal prosecutions. Previous winners include exiled Chinese artist

Today, we hear more and more news about torture by the police, people vanishing

Rebel Pepper, Syrian journalist Zaina Erhaim and Yemeni artist Murad Subay.

One of the nominations in the campaigning category this year is Team 29, an association of lawyers defending those whose free speech rights are threatened in Russia.

Ivan Pavlov, lawyer and head of Team 29, told Index that it was "a great honour for the whole Team 29 to be nominated for the

CREDIT: Taylor Callery/Ikon

Frightening state

47(01): 122/124 | DOI: 10.1177/0306422018769586

Governments are kidnapping journalists and their families to stop them reporting on stories they don't want covered, **Jemimah Steinfeld** writes

UGANDAN JOURNALIST CHARLES Etukuri had just left the office and was on his way to lunch when he was kidnapped in February. Working for daily newspaper New Vision, he believes his abduction was because of an article he wrote detailing the death of a Finnish national in Kampala.

Etukuri was surrounded by men in military uniform as he got into his car. He was handcuffed, taken to an undisclosed location and held for six days. He told Index he was tortured and that he feared for his life. While in custody, his captors demanded that he reveal the sources behind the story, but he refused. They let him go only after they had gone through all his private emails.

Today he still doesn't feel safe, saying he is being trailed and that his phone is being tapped. He communicated with Index over the encrypted WhatsApp service.

"There are usually procedures to be followed when summoning journalists... We are now being intimidated," he said.

Etukuri believes the problem lies with a few government officials in the security department. "It's saddening that the president, who fought for the establishing rule of law, is silent."

Etukuri is the second high-profile journalist to have been kidnapped in Uganda in the past six months. Freelance journalist Isaac Bakka disappeared in October last year, and it was only this February that news of Bakka's imprisonment emerged, following months of inquiries from his immediate family. He is charged with high treason.

The kidnapping of journalists is not unique to Uganda. Across the world we are seeing journalists and writers who dare to criticise those in power disappear.

Index spoke to Aasim Saeed, a blogger from Pakistan who now lives in the UK. Saeed was kidnapped and held in captivity for 21 days last year, suffering emotional and physical abuse. He joins a cohort of abducted journalists and dissidents in Pakistan.

According to the Human Rights Commission of Pakistan, since 2011 there have been more than 3,500 such disappearances. Saeed said his kidnapping departed from the past pattern in his area of Punjab because it was carried out by state forces rather than extremists.

"Previously if you were a journalist you would be beaten on the road or you would be threatened to keep you silent. Abduction is an extreme thing they've started doing," said Saeed.

In some cases, when it's not possible to target the journalists directly, close family members are kidnapped instead.

This tactic can be seen in the example of Chinese-American journalist Chen Xiaoping, whose wife was kidnapped in China last September. In January, a video of her emerged,

His captors demanded that he reveal the sources behind the story

in which she said she cut off all contact with Chen due to "emotional issues" and his "overseas work".

"It's clear that my wife's kidnapping and my work have been totally related," Chen said in response. His crime? Writing about corruption in the upper echelons of the Chinese Communist Party.

The message is loud and clear: governments don't just want to punish those who bad-mouth them, they want to scare people so much they won't pick up pen and paper.

It's a tactic the team at Radio Free Asia know all too well. Four staff members who report from Washington on China's draconian presence in Xinjiang have seen their close relatives detained. Three of RFA journalist Shohret Hoshur's brothers have been arrested. One still remains in prison.

Both Etukuri and Saeed fear for their families, too.

"Before I was freed, my family received →

→ messages threatening their lives. Since I've left, my parents are still visited," said Saeed. His parents have asked him to keep a low profile, for their safety as much as his. "I'm still writing, but in a subtle, not very blunt way," he added.

Etukuri said his home has been attacked and his family harassed.

"My dogs chased them away, but the next day they broke into my car," he said.

When it's not possible to target the journalists directly, close family members are kidnapped instead

Adding fuel to the fire is technology. Advances in tracking phones and computers, alongside the global and undeletable nature of the internet, mean it's increasingly easy to trace the movements of journalists and their families. These sophisticated detection tools are combining with the more familiar, cruder methods of silencing people – and the results are toxic.

"They have gone as far as basically saying 'We know where you live. We have your telephone numbers. We know where your children go to school. We know who and where your family is'," said Melinda Quintos de Jesus, a veteran Filipino journalist, in an interview with Vice magazine.

"You know that you have been watched – not just by ordinary people who hate you but [by] people who have the power to investigate and to track you, and to know where you are," she said.

This toxic combination also means no one is immune, and the days when journalists could seek sanctuary elsewhere appear to be coming to an end. Big Brother is borderless, and regimes successfully portray themselves as omnipresent, with the ability to spy – and seize people – anywhere in the world.

Guo Wengui, the Chinese businessman interviewed by Chen who incriminated the Communist Party, said he was pursued by Chinese security officers in New York. Afghan Mukhtarli, a journalist living in Tbilisi, Georgia, was kidnapped there last year and resurfaced in his home country, Azerbaijian. He was investigating the assets of the Azerbaijan president's family in Georgia, according to a Facebook post by a colleague.

Some of those who are kidnapped are released, others are not. The body of disappeared Honduran journalist Ángel Alfredo Villatoro Rivera was found last May. His murder occurred a week after another kidnapped Honduran journalist, Erick Martinez Ávila, was also found dead. Then there is the list of journalists who aren't even kidnapped, just killed outright, such as Slovakian journalist Jan Kuciak, who was shot dead alongside his girlfriend in his apartment at the end of February.

And for those who survive, the trauma does not end upon release. Speaking to Yemeni journalist, cameraman and filmmaker Abdulaziz Muhammad al-Sabri, he explained that he continues to be affected "psychologically and negatively to this day" and has "had difficulties recovering from it".

Al-Sabri was kidnapped twice, in one instance being held in chains for 15 days. His laptop and camera were also destroyed.

He said he can't go back to work, in part because of the trauma and in part because he no longer has equipment.

The fear that incidents such as these instil in those still living and working in areas where kidnappings occur is evident and, as al-Sabri's example shows, it is driving people away from working for the media.

One journalist from China, who wished to remain anonymous, said he had recently left the industry and did not expect to return anytime soon. When asked why, he responded bluntly. "What's the point?" ⊗

Jemimah Steinfeld is the deputy editor of Index on Censorship